Stations of the Crib
A JOURNEY OF HOPE
FROM ADVENT TO EPIPHANY

"When we hear of the stations, we think of Good Friday. Not necessarily anymore! Here are a new set of stations, stopping off places of hope. Instead of journeying in heart and soul to the cross, we go to the crib. Instead of Jerusalem, we go to Bethlehem. Joe Nassal is our guide, pointing out the markers of hope along the way. Some stations are familiar: annunciation, visitation, nativity. But some will set you mulling and wondering: magnification, declaration, evasion, nomination among others. There are fifteen in all, as you tread your way through Luke and Matthew's stories of expectation and birth and all that swirls around this child who is coming into history and hearts. The pattern is familiar…a moment of adoration, a meditation on a portion of scripture accompanied by a delightful story that will stick with you in a phrase or a line of dialogue and solid theology to stick to your guts, probing and asking how you travel, or are you aware of the company you keep and what's going on in this crazy world around us. It is rare to have such good theology that pushes us towards silence and turns us towards attentive prayer, in words that turn us soundlessly towards the One who leaps down from the night sky in stillness as deep and loud as stars falling. This is a singularly innovative way to do the season of Advent, Christmas and Epiphany this year and begin a tradition that will last through many generations. Joe Nassal has given the church a gift, a new devotion rich in scripture and contemporary meaning."

—**Megan McKenna**, author, *Prophets, Words of Fire*, theologian, storyteller, wayfarer, ambassador of peace for Pax Christi

"Taking his inspiration from the Stations of the Cross, Joe Nassal provides the reader deeply thoughtful meditations on the events and message of the infancy gospels. There is a strong connection between the events of the passion of Jesus and the marvelous events of his origin — both dimensions of Christ's life point to the heart of the gospel. Exquisitely written, these meditations on the gospel accounts are not abstract but find the gospel message in the lives and experiences of everyday Christians. Readers will find here strong food for the soul."

—**Donald Senior**, C.P., President of Catholic Theological Union, general editor of the acclaimed *Catholic Study Bible*, author, *Jesus, A Gospel Portrait* and *The Gospel of Matthew*

Stations of the Crib

A Journey of Hope
from Advent to Epiphany

Joseph Nassal, CPPS

Forest of Peace
Publishing

Suppliers for the Spiritual Pilgrim
Leavenworth, KS

Other Books by the Author:
(available from Forest of Peace Publishing)

The Conspiracy of Compassion
Rest Stops for the Soul
Premeditated Mercy
Moments of Truth

Stations of the Crib

Library of Congress Cataloging-in-Publication Data

Nassal, Joe, 1955-
  Stations of the crib : a journey of hope from Advent to Epiphany /
Joseph Nassal.
    p. cm.
  ISBN 0-939516-64-0
  1. Advent—Meditations. 2. Christmas—Meditations. 3.
  Epiphany—Meditations. I. Title.
  BX2170.A4 N37 2002
  242'.33—dc21

                                                    2002013269

published by

Forest of Peace Publishing, Inc.
PO Box 269
Leavenworth, KS 66048-0269   USA
1-800-659-3227
www.forestofpeace.com

printed by

Hall Commercial Printing
Topeka, KS 66608-0007

1st printing: September 2002

Dedication

To my sisters,
Sharon and Mary,
and my brother, Bob,
with gratitude
for your love and friendship.
Through the years,
in the laughter and the tears
you have taught me how to be
a seeker of hope.

Contents

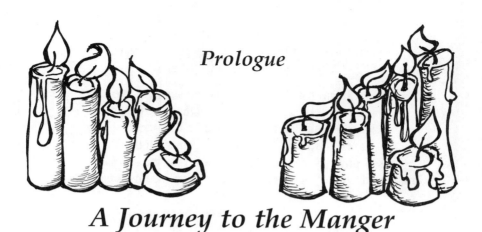

Prologue

A Journey to the Manger

PUTTING HOPE ON THE MAP

A few days before Christmas last year
I was making my way across the desert of Arizona.
I got off the interstate and followed a road
that led from the desert to the mountains.
Along the way I went through a town called Hope.
There is nothing in Hope except a service station
and a café that doubles as an antique store.
It is so small that Hope is not even on the map.

The landscape looked bleak,
but the people who live in Hope have a sense of humor.
Not only do they call their town "Hope"
in what seems a God-forsaken part of the world;
they also have posted a sign about a mile out of town.
The sign says, "You are now beyond Hope."

This book seeks to confirm the belief
that we are never beyond hope.

Just when we seem lost
and loitering uneasily at the edge of despair,
God shows us the way to hope.

A child born in a manger on the outskirts of the city
"because there was no room for them in the inn"
provides the map to show the world the way to hope.
This child "wrapped in swaddling cloths"
will unwrap and reveal the real presence of God
in a world where too often hate, not hope, seems victorious.
This child will create quite a stir —
making his unborn cousin dance
in the ancient womb of his mother,
causing a humble young woman to sing
and an old man to lose and then find his voice.
This child will cause angels to appear out of nowhere,
shepherds to leave their flocks and scamper to an out-of-the-way place
and wise ones weary from the road to feel right at home.
This child will cause a young carpenter to dream and craft a life of faith
and an old couple to find their life's fulfillment in God's Word.
And a king, fearful of the presence of this child,
will unleash a reign of terror.
But this child will show to a world where terrorism
threatens to take an upper hand
the "tender hand of our God."

This book was born during a time of sabbatical
granted to me by my religious community.
My entire Sabbath time, blessed as it was,
took place under a cloud of terrorism.
I left my previous assignment in Ruma, Illinois,
on September 10, 2001.
On September 11, "all hell broke loose"

with the terrorists attacks
in New York, Washington and Pennsylvania.
What happened on September 11 showed us yet again
the presence of evil in the world.
These "Stations of the Crib" celebrate God's response to this evil.
God responds to darkness by becoming light.
God responds to hate by becoming love.
God responds to despair by daring the people of the earth
to hope again in the divine presence
in the world and in themselves.

In the tradition of the Stations of the Cross,
the devotion spiritual pilgrims
have used for centuries during Lent
to prepare for observing the events of Holy Week
and the celebration of Easter,
this book offers fifteen stations drawn from
the Infancy Narratives in the Gospel of Luke
and the beginning of Matthew's Gospel.
We hear these familiar Scripture passages
from the beginning of Advent
through the celebration of Epiphany
when God dares us to hope again.

It is my hope that these Stations of the Crib
that mark the way to the manger
and the mission that lies beyond it
might remind us of the intimate connection
between the events surrounding Jesus' birth
and those of his suffering, death and resurrection.
We cannot separate the crib from the cross.
The way to the manger mirrors
the way of the cross.

There is an old saying,
"God is in the heavens and all's right with the world."
But when terrorists target twin towers,
killing thousands of innocent people
and the world is at war,
everything is not right with the world.

So God comes to earth.

This book celebrates how God is no longer just in the heavens
but how God comes down to earth
to make sure that when everything seems wrong
and the forces of evil threaten to extinguish hope,
God is right in the thick of things.

And with God in our midst,
we are never beyond hope.

February 28, 2002
Berkeley, CA

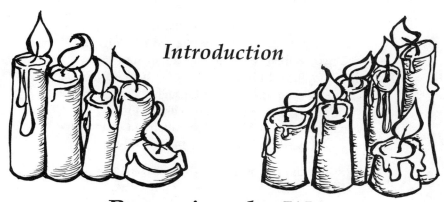

Introduction

Preparing the Way

STOPPING ALONG THE ADVENT WAY

Advent comes along at the time of year
when everyone seems to be in a hurry.
Though surrounded by many signs
that announce the birth of Christ,
most of these tend to seduce us into spending
more money on Christmas shopping
rather than spending more time in Advent stopping.
The pace and panic of the manic days before Christmas
are so contrary to the spirit of Advent.
Yet most of us, sooner or later,
fall victim to the hustle and bustle of this time of year —
until some event comes along that slows us down
and stops us in our tracks.

In the news a few years ago there was a story
about two women Christmas shopping with their children.
When they had finished shopping,
they loaded their gifts in the trunk and their children in the back seat

and set off for home.
As they were speeding along the freeway,
the two women were talking in the front seat.
Suddenly, they heard the children in the back seat scream
and the whistle of the wind coming through the open back door.
Quickly they turned and to their horror
saw that one of the children had fallen out of the car
and was tumbling along the freeway.

The mother of the child was driving.
In her terror, she slammed on the brakes.
Both women jumped out of the car and ran toward the child.
When they arrived at her motionless body,
they noticed something extraordinary.
All of the traffic of this busy freeway had stopped.
The cars were lined up like a parking lot.
A car had not hit the child.
In fact, the car that would have hit her had stopped
just a few feet short of the child.
When the women arrived at the scene,
a large man was bending over the little girl.
"She's still alive," he said. "Let's get her to a hospital."
The man was a truck driver, and he picked up the child
while the two mothers and the rest of the children climbed into his truck.
When they arrived at the hospital,
the child was unconscious but still breathing.

In the emergency room,
the doctors and nurses began checking her vital signs.
In the hushed waiting room,
the truck driver and a few of the folks who had stopped on the freeway
and followed them to the hospital sat with the mother of the child
who had fallen out of the car.

After what seemed like a very long time,
one of the doctors came into the room and told the mother
that her child was going to be okay.
She had several bruises and abrasions but no broken bones
as a result of her vicious tumble along the freeway.

This story offers a road sign as we begin this journey of hope.
It is a sign many of us might miss
because the days and weeks before Christmas
we are busy about many things.
Our lives resemble a race on a speedway
rather than a leisurely stroll in the slow lane.

But then a door flies open and a child tumbles from safety
into the path of a rushing world.
For those coming from behind,
this child appears on the highway out of nowhere,
almost as if she has fallen from the sky.
Suddenly, the rushing world comes to a stop,
for a child is now in the path of our high-speed chase
to get to where we are going.
A child brings the world to a standstill.
The race stops.
A child is in the way.

May this small book of reflections
help us to resist the temptation to rush around
and instead step on the brake,
slow the pace
and make some space.
There's a child in the middle of the road
and his name is Jesus, the incarnation of God's Hope.
He is the One who makes us hope seekers.

Prayer: Hope Is in the Way

Holy and Beloved God,
we are grateful for the gift of hope
you have placed in the middle of our Advent way
in the person of your Son, Jesus Christ.
In the wilderness of our ancestors' exile,
your prophet foretold of a new road,
a highway of holiness,
weaving through the wasteland of their lives,
offering them a new avenue to the promised land.

In lives crowded with despair,
cluttered with broken dreams,
your prophet tells us to make way for the coming of our God.
John burst upon this wilderness scene
proclaiming new possibilities of repentance and renewal
for those whose hope had grown old.
He invites us to slow the pace
and move in the rhythm of your redeeming grace.

This is the season, O Gracious God,
when you invite us to begin again;
to believe again in the promise of your prophets.
On this Advent avenue,
give us the courage to give comfort to those we meet.
Grant us patience to stand and wait,
to watch and to pray on this Advent way.
Nurture the hope within us
that will afford us the vision
to see the beginning of a new day
for all your people.

+ *Amen.*

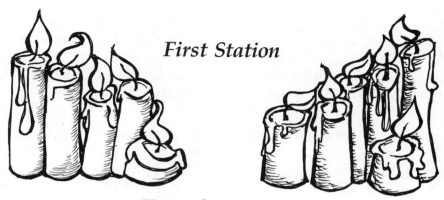

Proclamation

HOPE: ROOTED IN MEMORY

In the days of Herod, King of Judea,
there was a priest named Zechariah...
Luke 1: 5

At the time I met Frank,
he was 94 years old and living alone in a house
his grandfather built more than 100 years before.
The house sat on one acre of land surrounded by the university,
which took nine of the ten acres Frank once owned to make a parking lot.

Though Frank didn't see as well as he used to, his mind was sharp.
He once was a journalist and a professor at a university in Chicago.
He kept up on current events, as evidenced by the newsmagazine
open on the table next to his chair.
I remember a magnifying glass lying on top of a story about the fall
of the Berlin Wall, which happened a couple of weeks before I met Frank.
That magnifying glass kept Frank in touch with his world.

After teaching for many years, Frank settled down to write.
With more than a hint of humility, Frank called himself a "hack" writer.
"Otherwise," he said, "you would have heard of me."
But the old, battered Royal typewriter sitting on his kitchen table
showed that Frank still wrote the most important prose of all:
letters to friends and relatives.

I listened to Frank unravel story after story.
Near the end of our visit, he said,
"You know, Father, when I die, this land goes to the church.
Maybe they could build the new church here —
you know the one we have now is just too small."
Frank's eyes sparkled at the thought.

Later, I thought about all that Frank had seen through his aging eyes
during the 94 years of his life —
all the wars and repression and depression,
the advances of science and the anguish of human suffering,
the tragedies and triumphs of almost a century.
I stood in awe and with a sense of amazement and admiration.

Here was a man for all seasons, but especially for the season of hope.
Because for all the changes, all the pain, all the promise of his years,
Frank had kept his hope alive.

HOPE: MEMORY OF THE FUTURE

Somewhere inside every human heart,
either so near the surface that you need only scratch to see it,
or buried so deep inside that it takes years to uncover,
there is a longing, a dreaming, a yearning for a better future.
For Frank, it was the hope that when he died
his land would be used by the parish to build
a dwelling place for his faith community.

The story of the Incarnation is about making sure
that when God comes to earth, God has a place to stay.
God's house-hunting begins with an old couple, Zechariah and Elizabeth,
who are told they will be the proud parents of the prophet
who will prepare the way for God's latest adventure in real estate.
Just as once upon a time God chose an elderly couple way past their prime,
telling Abraham and Sarah
they would be the parents of countless generations,
so God now chooses Zechariah and Elizabeth
to further the divine plan of salvation.

This plan involves relocation.
In real estate, location is everything.
Evidently when it comes to real presence, location leads to salvation.
This First Station suggests how our homeless God is in search of a home —
or, more precisely, that God is looking to make a home on earth.
God is not looking for an apartment — to live apart from human beings.
Nor is God looking for a dwelling made of mortar and brick.
God is in the market for flesh and blood.
God wants to make the divine home in the human heart.

As we might expect, Zechariah is troubled
by the visit of this angelic real estate agent.
The angel doesn't go into detail with Zechariah
about God's housing plan of salvation.
Suffice it to say that this is not "urban development"
but an astonishing divine development.
It is not "urban renewal" but the renewal of the face of the earth.

This sounds too good to be true, and so Zechariah asks, "How can this be?"
This question — sound as it may be for the old priest to ask —
would be the last sound Zechariah would make for a while,
as he is struck speechless by these amazing developments.

When he questions the veracity of the angelic visitation,
Zechariah is dumbfounded.
Can we blame him?
Have you ever heard news that left you speechless?
Or an event that so overwhelmed you that you couldn't speak?
Or an experience so awe-inspiring that it moved you beyond words?

Zechariah lost his voice because his trust that God would keep
the divine promises was wearing thin.
Doubt nibbled at the fringes of his soul, as he says to the angel Gabriel:
"How am I to know this?
I am an old man; my wife, too, is advanced in age."

This is the way God works:
from that which was thought to be worn out and weary,
too old or too barren, doomed and near death,
new life emerges.
As with Abraham and Sarah, so it is with Zechariah and Elizabeth:
from these roots of our memory, hope is born.

But Zechariah could not find the confidence to believe
in this possibility of such a miracle occurring in his life.
And for his lack of confidence,
his lack of trust in God performing a miracle
in what had become the routine of his retirement years,
Zechariah was told by the messenger of God's good news,
"You will be mute — unable to speak —
until the day when these things take place."
He was rendered silent because he had his doubts
about God's new real estate development,
this divine plan of relocation.

When the news is too good to be true,
maybe silence is the only appropriate response.

The news that he would be a father left Zechariah speechless.
This news would change his life — and the life of the world — forever.
It was too good to be true.

We should not be surprised Zechariah found himself dumb.
Don't we say, "I can't put into words how I feel,"
or "What I am feeling now is beyond words."
When we are dumbfounded, let Zechariah be our interpreter.

This First Station is not a time for making speeches
but a time to be speechless.
It is a time to be dumbfounded, to sit still and be quiet,
to walk and talk softly and carry a big heart.
Advent is the time
hope seekers allow God to do the talking.
And God will speak the Word that will become flesh
and dwell among us.
This news will move us beyond words.
It will leave us speechless.

HOPE IN THE PAST

Hope not only focuses on the future;
it is also found in the way we view our past.
Toward the end of poet Robert Frost's life, someone asked him,
"Do you have hope for the future?"
Frost paused and then said, "Yes, and even for the past."

It's true: Hope is a virtue
not only reserved for our pondering about the future.
Hope is the virtue that helps us come to terms with our past.
The poet had hope for the past
"that it will turn out to have been all right for what it was."
When we apply hope to our past,

we find it something that we can accept.

Mistakes that we made once upon a time
were made by who we were then,
who we had to be at that time in our lives.
We may wish we were someone else when we made these mistakes.
We may have prayed that we were better people at the time,
that our hearts were larger and our love wider.
But we were who we were at the time.
Mistakes were made; missed opportunities occurred.
There's nothing we can do about that now except hope
"that it will turn out to have been all right."

Why spend half our time living in the past — or trying to relive it —
when all we really need to do is to reverence the past and hope in it?
We all have regrets. We all have made mistakes.
We all find ourselves now and then
wishing we hadn't said or done this or that.
We all find ourselves at times
wishing we had not moved to that place or left that other place.
We all wish we had stayed in touch a little more
with the people we left behind.

There will always be regrets.
But hope in the past allows us to pitch a wide tent
at every corner of God's creation.
A tent so large that all people might find
shelter from the storms of life.
A tent so expansive that people who start on the wings of our lives,
the right wing and the left wing,
might "wing" their way home
and find a safe place in the center of our hearts.

When God decided to pitch the divine tent on earth,

God made every corner of every piece of land,
of every avenue or expressway,
of every driveway or speedway,
of every field ripe with grain
and every field covered with concrete
holy ground.
Under this divine tent
those who have been forsaken and forgotten
find a new friend.
Under this tent,
those who live in the past,
those who are burdened by life, by illness, by anger,
by grief, by guilt, by shame or by blame,
might find a new hope.
A hope for the past — that it is something we can bear,
something we can carry,
something we can use to build an even larger tent.

We pitch our tent in this holy place
where God's mercy and grace invites us to forgo regret
as we hope not only in the future but also in our past.

Frank had decided that even though his life was almost over,
there was no looking back at the past.
Rather, he treasured the precious moments of his life
and wanted to pass on to his parish, his friends,
a legacy of love.
This old man, well past his prime,
wanted his community of faith to relocate on the land he left behind.
This is the stuff of vision.
When we take the time to trace the genealogy of grace
that pulses throughout our personal history,
we give birth to a future full of hope.

God has pitched the divine tent in our camp,
in each of our hearts.
Our pilgrim God has settled in each of our souls.
God does indeed dwell among us.
And when God dwells among us,
then we dwell in possibility, because nothing
is impossible with God.

First Station Prayer

We adore you, O Christ, and we bless you,
because by your holy birth you give hope to the world.

Gracious God,
accompany me now as I take a stroll down memory lane.
Allow me to look through the rearview mirror of my life
to see etched on every experience your promise:
"Objects are closer than they appear."

You are always closer to me than it first appears.
As I look in the rearview mirror of memory
and recall your love for me and all your people,
I find comfort and consolation.

Your proclamation of a future full of hope
to an old and weary priest
tested his faith and moved him to silence.
I move to a stance of silence at this station
as I remember how your promises are never empty
but always full of hope.

As you sustain me by helping me to touch again
the stories of your fidelity to me throughout my life,
help me to sustain others by becoming
a living proclamation of your promises fulfilled.

+Amen.

Second Station

Annunciation

WAKE-UP CALL

*In the sixth month the angel Gabriel was sent from God
to a city of Galilee named Nazareth,
to a virgin betrothed to a man whose name was Joseph,
of the house of David;
and the virgin's name was Mary.*
Luke 1: 26-27

In the story *Through the Looking-Glass,*
Lewis Carroll's sequel to his classic,
Alice's Adventures in Wonderland,
Alice looks through a mirror hanging above the fireplace
and suddenly finds herself once again in a magical land.
Among the characters she meets are Humpty-Dumpty,
Tweedledee and Tweedledum, the White Knight and the Queen of Hearts.
At one point Alice says to the queen,
"There's no use trying, one can't believe impossible things."
"I daresay you haven't had much practice," the queen replies.

"When I was your age,
I always did it for half-an-hour a day.
Why, sometimes I've believed
as many as six impossible things before breakfast."

Mary might have smiled at the Queen's advice to Alice.
After all, Mary had to believe
in the most impossible thing of all before breakfast —
that she would be the mother of the Messiah.
But then the angel told her that for those who believe,
"all things are possible with God."

At the beginning of Luke's Gospel,
Gabriel is a busy angel.
First he appears to Zechariah and says,
"Do not be afraid, for your prayer is heard,
and your wife Elizabeth will bear you a son,
and you shall call his name John."
Then Gabriel appears to Mary
and uses almost the same line:
"Do not be afraid, for you have found favor with God.
And behold, you will conceive in your womb
and bear a son, and you shall call his name Jesus."
It is as if Gabriel is working from a cosmic cue card
and fills in the blank with the name of the child
that goes to the parent he is appearing to at the time.

Gabriel, who plays an important role in these first two stations,
invites us to consider how we entertain the idea of angels.

ANGELS: GOD'S ALARM CLOCKS

Angels serve an important purpose for those in search of hope.
In Scripture, angels seem to serve as God's alarm clocks,

waking and shaking the people to whom they are sent
out of their deep slumber and into a deeper commitment.

A quick glance at angelic conversations in Scriptures
reflects that the language of angels repeatedly evokes the challenge to
"wake up."
The angel said to Gideon, "Arise and go."
The angel said to Elijah, "Arise and eat."
The angel who appeared to Peter in prison told him, "Wake up, go."
The angel said to Joseph, "Wake up, do not be afraid."
Jacob wrestled with an angel during a long night,
while Mary welcomed one at morning's first light.
Both of their encounters changed their lives forever.

Though Scripture is full of such stories,
stock in angels probably began to fall when theologians began arguing
about how many angels can dance on the head of a pin.
Rational people scoffed at such superstitious silliness,
and angels seemed to visit the earth less frequently.
When we were in grade school our teachers always told us
to leave enough room in our seat for our guardian angel.
But as we grew up, we began taking up more room,
and angels were squeezed out to take their place
in the closet reserved for pious relics.

Now angels are making a comeback.
An entire section at Barnes & Noble
is reserved for books about angels,
as writers seek to bring the transcendent down to earth.
Angel awareness seminars draw large crowds,
while CDs of angelic sounds seek to lift the spirits
of earthly dwellers to heavenly heights.
People have been watching stories of being *Touched by an Angel*

on television for many years now.
Even the U.S. Postal System responded to the renewed interest in
angels by capturing their visage on stamps,
perhaps in hopes that mail delivery
might be speeded up on the wings of angels
(which, of course, gives a whole new meaning to "air mail").

Maybe the reason angels are coming out of the closet today
is because for too long we lost our sense of wonder.
We lost our sense of the sacred.
We lost our sense of childlike belief.
And now society in general is so scarred by cynicism,
so worn and tired and confused,
that we are trying to recapture
the innocence and trust of our childhood.

Perhaps the comeback of angels is reminding us
that we can't do it on our own;
we need God's intervention.

This truth is evoked in the prayer that for many Roman Catholics
was probably the first prayer we ever learned.
Kneeling at the side of our bed,
hands folded, eyes closed, the words came without pause:
"Angel of God, my guardian dear,
to whom God's love commits me near.
Ever this day be at my side,
to light, to guard, to rule and guide."
The words come to mind without thinking.
They are forever engraved on my memory.
It is a prayer of comfort and consolation,
a prayer for protection and guidance.
The sentiment expressed in that simple prayer

does not have to become so sentimental that it loses its strength.
Rather, it may remind us how God desires to intervene
to "light, to guard, to rule and guide"
all the events of our day.

Room to Wait, Wake and See

While keeping us awake —
or waking us up if our souls have been asleep —
angels also serve as chamberlains or bellhops to provide room service.

This station celebrates how God, communicating through an angel,
prepared a place in Mary's body for the Divine Presence to dwell.
Mary received God's Word made flesh
so that the new covenant may dwell within us.
Unlike the ancient Ark of the Covenant that,
according to the book of Revelation,
"was seen within the temple,"
this new covenant dwells within us.
We carry the Divine Presence in the ark of our hearts,
inside our bodies.

Provided, of course, there is room.

Too often there is so much stuff that clutters the ark of our hearts
that it is a challenge for God's angels to find enough room
to make God's self at home.

This Second Station raises the question of room:
Is there room to wait and see?
At this station we are in the waiting room,
filled with expectation and anticipation.
Some of us pace back and forth
as we await the birth of redeeming grace.

Some of us sit still, with eyes closed,
to catch the first glimpse or glimmer of light
piercing the darkness of night.
Some of us frantically try to tie up loose ends —
either on gifts that we've bought for relatives or friends
or loose ends of relationships that have unraveled over time.

However we spend these few weeks in the waiting room,
it's a time to sense how this light of Christ is growing within us.
It's time to sense the presence of the light that takes the chill off
these cold winter days and nights,
to sense the fire of love from family and friends
that warms our hands and hearts
with the true message of this grace period,
this time of waiting, waking, seeing.

Listen for the alarm clock ringing in our hearts: Wake up!
Hear this clear and certain warning: Keep awake!
We are not to allow the routine of our lives to lull us to sleep.
We are not to allow regrets over past mistakes to make us drowsy.
We are not to allow mundane tasks that crowd our days
to cause us to grow sluggish, listless and lethargic.

The kind of wakefulness this station advises
is not so much for the body as it is for the soul.
Our bodies need rest. We need our sleep.
When we are deprived of sufficient sleep,
we can become manic and prone to panic attacks.
As seekers of hope,
we are not to stock up on No-Doz
or fuel our bodies with enough caffeine to keep us on edge.
Rather, we are advised to make certain our souls are awake and alert
so that when the One in whom we hope stands at our door,

we are ready to welcome him home
and ensure he finds more than enough room
to stay for a while.

This station offers ample waiting room,
room to wait and see.
But if we're in a "rush," we are not going to take kindly
to the suggestion that we "wait and see."
That is why this practice is more difficult than it seems.
Many of us wake up and are ready to go.
"Wake, wait and see" has been replaced by
"Ready, set, go!"
Taking a "wait and see" attitude in this day and age doesn't fly.
Only time and angels fly.

But a person who adopts a wait and see attitude
understands that time is not within one's power to control.
We may think we have all the time in the world,
but only God knows what time it is.
That is why we stay awake and wait and see,
for we don't know when our time will come.

We adopt this wait and see attitude toward life
not because we are cautiously optimistic
but because we are bold in our belief
that all will be well in the end.
This is the quality of hope these stations seek to teach us.
It is God who keeps awake,
who adopts a wait and see attitude toward us.

'Tis the season not of cautious optimism but of bold hope.
It is a season when we can wake, wait and see
the wonders God has in store for us.
And this store is always open.

There is no rush.
Hope is always in stock.
Just wait and see.

Just as God had a special plan
for Mary's child and Elizabeth's child,
God has a special plan for each of us.
In the waiting room of these days and nights
before we celebrate the birth of Mary's child,
it is time to stir the flame of faith, of hope, of love,
to recapture the dream and recover the destiny.

Second Station Prayer

We adore you, O Christ, and we bless you,
because by your holy birth you give hope to the world.

God of Impossible Dreams,
Awaken in me a childlike spirit of trust
to believe that with you at the center of my life
all things are possible.

Mary, Mother of the greatest dreamer
the world has ever known,
be my companion at this station
as I hear the angel's words to you:
"Do not be afraid."
With your life, Blessed Mary,
you announced faith in God's dreams for you
and the courage to live in hope.

Make me, O God, a messenger of hope today.
As you send your messengers
"to light, to guard, to rule and guide"
all our days and all our nights,
increase my awareness of your presence.
You are with us always, O God.
And in your presence,
all dreams come true.

+Amen.

Provided by the Maryknoll sisters
of the San Salvador Diocesan HIV/AIDS programme

God of all compassion,
Comfort your sons and daughters
Who live with HIV.
Spread over us all your quilt of Mercy,
Love and Peace.

Open our eyes to your presence
Reflected in their faces.
Open our ears to your truth
Echoing in their hearts.

Give us the strength
To weep with the grieving,
To walk with the lonely,
To stand with the depressed.

May our love mirror your love
For those who live in fear,
Who live under stress and
Who suffer rejection.

Mothering, fathering God
Grant rest to those who have died
And hope to all who live with HIV.

God of life, help us to find the cure now
And help us to build a world in which
No one dies alone and where
Everyone lives accepted
Wanted and loved.

Third Station

Visitation

Batteries Not Included

In those days, Mary arose and went with haste
into the hill country, to a city of Judah,
and she entered the house of Zechariah and Elizabeth.
Luke 1: 39-40

Mary and Elizabeth take center stage at this Third Station.
The relationship of these two women
is one that leaves a mark on our soul.
Two women — one too old to have a baby
and the other too young —
reach out to one another with love
because God has reached out to them.
God has chosen these two women to give birth to the future.
As they await the birth of their sons,
they will hold on to one another for dear life —
the life growing within their wombs.
They will help one another and hope in one another.

Here is a modern parable
based on these two women of hope:

The old woman pulled the collar of her worn overcoat
close around her neck.
The bus station was cold and damp.
She tried to hide herself in the crowd of people
trying to get out of town and home for the holidays.
She found an empty seat and watched some of the frantic faces
whose eyes seemed to strain to read the small letters
on the monitor listing departures.
This old woman spent her life watching,
because keeping watch was a good way to wait
for whatever might happen next.
She watched the people respond Pavlov-like
to the announcements of departures that came over the loudspeakers.
Yes, it was a busy night at the bus station.
And as long as the station was crowded,
she could hide there quite well.

At one point, though, the crowd thinned out a bit,
and she noticed a younger woman sitting by herself at the lunch counter.
The old woman watched her a while and noticed that
the only thing this younger woman was watching was her cup of coffee.
As the old woman checked her pockets,
she figured the girl was 18 or 19 years old at the most.
Finding some change deep in her coat pockets,
the old woman got up and walked toward the counter.

"Gotta light?"
the old woman asked as she stood behind the younger woman.
Without looking up,
the younger one picked up her lighter from the counter

and held it over her shoulder.
The old one took the lighter and sat down next to the girl.
She flicked the lighter and said, "Oh, I forgot. I don't smoke."
But after ordering a cup of coffee,
the old woman kept flicking the lighter and watching the tiny flame.
Then she said, "They didn't tell you, did they?"

The younger woman looked at her.
"Didn't tell me what?"
"They didn't tell you that the batteries are not included."
"I don't know what you're talking about."
"Life, dear," the old woman said.
"Nobody told you that in life
the batteries aren't included."

The young girl remained silent.
The old woman sipped her coffee for a while.
"You headin' home for Christmas?" the old woman asked.
"I was," the girl replied. "My bus left an hour ago."
"So, you missed your bus? I'm sure there's another...."
"I didn't miss it," the girl said. "I was here. I just didn't get on it."

The old woman took another sip of coffee.
"My name's Liz," she said finally. "What's yours?"
"Lucy."

"What's wrong, Lucy? Why did you miss your bus?
Don't you want to go home?"
Lucy looked at Liz's face.
Her eyes seemed sincere.
"I can't go home," she said.

"Oh, honey, everyone can go home.
Remember what old Frosty — the poet, not the snowman — said,

'Home is the place that when you go there they have to take you in.' "
Lucy recognized the line from the Robert Frost poem
she studied in Freshmen English.
"Well, I doubt if old Frosty was ever in my situation."

Sensing that Lucy was warming up to her,
Liz decided to take the plunge.
"Now, what can be so bad that you can't go home?"

"I'm pregnant!"
Lucy blurted out these words
as if she would burst if she held them in any longer.
"My mom and dad are going to kill me."
"Oh, now, honey, I'm sure your mom and dad will understand."
"No, you're the one who doesn't understand.
You don't know my mom and dad."

After a long pause, Liz said,
"Well, you're right about that. I don't know them.
Still, I can't imagine them turning you away."

But Lucy was silent.
Liz flicked the lighter a few more times
as the clerk behind the counter poured more coffee.

The two women sat in silence for a while.
Finally, Liz said,
"Honey, I know your world seems pretty dark right now,
but it's only going to look a lot darker,
and feel a lot colder, the longer you stay in this bus station.
Why don't you go on home, honey?
Your parents just might surprise you.
After all, they must believe in you
or they wouldn't have given you such an old-fashioned name."

"What do you mean?"
"I don't hear a lot of girls being named Lucy these days," Liz said.
"You know what it means, don't you? It means 'light.'
Your mom and dad believe in you, Lucy.
So, you just go up to that ticket counter
and find out when the next bus leaves for home.
And you take that light home with you.
You take that life that is inside you home.
And even if there are times when even home seems dark and cold,
you just remember your name."
Liz flicked the lighter.
Then she handed it back to Lucy and said,
"Thanks for the light."

THE PRESENCE OF LIGHT

The story of Liz and Lucy is not so different
from the Gospel story about Mary and Elizabeth.
One is old, the other is young.
Both are pregnant — Lucy with a child, Liz with wisdom.
Could Mary have felt much differently than Lucy?
She was a young, unwed mother.
She had to be concerned what her parents would think;
how her fiancé, Joseph, would react.
But after the angel's invitation to believe
that God's promises would be fulfilled through her,
Mary didn't go home to tell her parents.
She didn't fill Joseph in on the details.
Instead, she went in haste to her wise cousin, Elizabeth —
to help her in her need,
to share the light that was within her womb
and shining through the windows of her soul.

At this Third Station, we celebrate the presence of the light
in a young woman named Mary.
We celebrate the presence of the light in an old woman, Elizabeth,
who was already sensitive to the light,
for when she heard Mary's greeting,
she felt the child within her womb take a leap of faith
and dance for joy.
These two women, Mary and Elizabeth,
remind all of us, female or male, young or old, rich or poor,
that we are all pregnant with the presence of God.

At this station, we touch the light that is inside each of us.
We take this light into a world so filled with traces of the night,
and we commit ourselves to share the light of love,
compassion, birth and beauty.
Advent comes during the darkest time of the year
in the Northern Hemisphere.
When the weather is so cold outside,
it is a good time to stay inside
and descend into the caves of our hearts.
Do we sense the presence of the light
that takes the chill off cold winter nights?
Do we sense on our skin the warmth of friends?
Do we feel God's favor filling us with the light of new promises to keep?
Are we pregnant with new possibilities for our future?

At this station on the way to the manger,
we are asked to believe in the light of our own goodness,
the light of God's truth growing within us.
In a young woman, unwed and wondering what all this means,
a light will stir.
In an old woman, barren and beyond hope,
a child will leap for joy.

A story will be told.
And the dark cave of the world
will become bright and warm
with the light of God's promise fulfilled.

Liz was right, you know.
Life comes along with the message,
"Batteries not included."
But that's okay, because when we feel run-down and tired,
overworked and underappreciated,
out of energy and out of time,
we find a spark, a story, a light
that glows from within the caves of our hearts.
And from this tiny, flickering flame,
we take our name and claim our future.
We pass the light on to someone still shivering in the dark,
afraid to go home.

As hope seekers,
we trust a new light will dawn.
In a young woman, unwed and wondering what all this means,
a light will stir.
In an old woman, barren and beyond hope,
a child will leap for joy.
In hearts broken by betrayal,
new hope will seep in and old hurts will leak out.
In minds clouded by doubt,
new faith will be kindled.

"Gotta light?"
Of course, we do.
We have lots of light.
So much light that all peoples of the earth
will be able to find their way home.

Third Station Prayer

We adore you, O Christ, and we bless you,
because by your holy birth you give hope to the world.

Blessed are you, O God,
and blessed are the holy women and men
through whom you manifest your Divine Presence.
You visit us each day in the holy and humble ones
we meet along the way.

In Mary and Elizabeth,
you reflect for our journey of hope
two wise women who never lost their sense of wonder
and always found your promises to them
fulfilled beyond their wildest dreams.

In the company of family and friends,
may we gather around the fire of your love
during this season of hope
to warm our bodies and souls on the sacred stories
of yesterday, today and tomorrow.

O Light of Lights,
make me a beacon of hope for someone in need.
Give me a light, O God,
so that when I get out of the way
and let your light shine through me,
another may find her/his way home.

+Amen.

Fourth Station

Magnification

Mary's Greatest Hit

And Mary said,
"My soul magnifies the Lord,
and my spirit rejoices in God my savior...."
Luke 1: 46-47

I don't know where I heard it or who said it,
but the words stay in my mind like lyrics of a song
that play over time until they are etched not in stone but in the soul.
The lyrics are:
"Hope is the ability to listen to the music of the future."

Mary listened to this music and became the mother of hope.
She is the greatest "soul" singer the world has known
because her soul magnified the hope God had in her.

This is Mary's greatest hit,
the number one song on the charts,
the tune that would capture the spirit of countless generations.

The Magnificat is a soulful melody that plays
in the hearts of believers throughout the centuries
and is played and prayed each evening in the Liturgy of the Hours.
Mary's song has become one of history's greatest hits
because it strikes a chord where we hurt and where we hope.

Perhaps the reason why we sing the Magnificat each evening
is because, like plodding prodigies just learning to the play the piano,
this is the only way we learn how to hope:
practice, practice, practice.
With the lyrics of hope offered in Mary's song,
this Fourth Station provides us some important pieces for our repertoire
to rehearse often until we know them by heart.
How can we practice the Magnificat's notes of hope?
By listening to and believing in the promise
that has already come in the person of Jesus
and will come again in glory.
The notes of this symphony of peace are already present in our lives.
So we practice this peace by sitting up straight
and hearing again the stirring of the Spirit in our souls.

In a world so often filled with the cacophony of crisis and chaos,
this station encourages us to practice the notes of hope daily
so that we can play a symphony of peace on the world's stage.

Where is there discord in our lives?
Where is there dissonance in our relationships with one another?
Where are our lives out of tune?
Where do we need to hear this music of hope?
In what relationships of our lives do we need
the fine-tuning of God's tender mercy?

We all know that when the melody of hope has become a dirge of despair,
it may take a long time to hear the harmony again.

At this station, we renew our commitment once again
to listen to and play this music of hope.
But hope takes practice.
Practice the notes of hope each day
until the melody is committed to memory.
Then let that music play.

A JOYFUL SONG

Though we hope our lives proclaim the greatness of our God,
we know our hurts can drown out the sound of hope.
Mary's song reminds us how to recognize
and realize the joy found in God our savior.

We cling to passing pleasures or past disappointments
and save them like souvenirs in the place that God
has reserved for the divine presence — the ark of our heart.
Passing pleasures can, for a time, ease the pain of past disappointments.
They can make us forget the hurt for a while.
But by their very nature and definition, they pass.

God desires that joy, not pleasure,
should take up residence in the ark of our hearts.
But we have our own reservations.
Do we really want our lives to radiate such joy?
Granted, many of us feel joy deep in our hearts
but fail to notify our faces.
It's like that old song,
"I've got joy, joy, joy deep down in my heart."
For some of us, the joy is buried so deep it rarely surfaces.
At this juncture on our way to the manger,
the message is simple and strong:
if we know joy in our hearts, let's please notify our faces!

Where is the joy in our life? When have we known joy?
In reflecting on these questions,
I believe there is a distinction to be made
between being happy and knowing joy.
In one of my parish assignments as a priest,
I was going through a very difficult time.
It seemed I was being confronted at every turn with my own limitations.
The failures were mounting and suffocating any semblance of success.
One day after Mass a friend looked at me and said:
"Joe, God wants us to be happy."

Now, she could have simply echoed the words of a song
that was popular at the time: "Don't worry, be happy."
But she was not suggesting superficial laughter or empty euphoria
to stem the tide of sorrow.
She did not say, "Cheer up, it could be worse."
She was reminding me of the divine desire for me to know joy.
God wants us to experience joy.

We discover this quality of joy
when we recognize that God is in our midst.
The world says, "Don't worry, be happy."
But the Word of God says, "Don't worry, rejoice!"
We can do this if we know how close our God is to us.

THE QUALITY OF JOY

The quality of joy that is evoked in Mary's song was reflected to me
in the face of a woman I met a few years ago.
Annette is the wife of a former classmate from the seminary.
As soon as I met her, I recognized her face.
We attended the same college, though she was a couple of years behind us.

Annette's smile reflected more than a cheerful disposition.

Her face reflected a sense of serenity.
I learned that Annette had suffered a number
of health problems the past few years.
She is an organ recipient, and that transplant has kept her alive.
The knowledge that she is alive because of the generosity of a donor
fills Annette's face with a gratitude.
Her whole being seems to proclaim the greatness of God.
So close to death, she is grateful for the gift of life.

Hearing the lyrics of Mary's song of joy on Annette's face that day,
it struck a chord within me: Have I ever known such joy?
Does my whole being proclaim the greatness of God?
Or is my life still cluttered with a string of souvenirs
of passing pleasures or past disappointments
rather than lasting joy?

Annette has found Mary's elusive joy
that comes through knowing that God alone is her Savior —
a God who was made manifest to her in the person
whose donor card or family gave her the gift of life.
This is the joy that forms the basic harmony in Mary's song,
a song whose lyrics profess the faith
that God's promises will be fulfilled.

Mary's Magnificat is a manifesto of faith
where the proud are confused while the humble see clearly,
where the mighty fall and the lowly rise,
where the rich find their pockets are empty
while the hungry are full of God.

Mary's Magnificat is the anthem for all those who know
that true joy comes not from filling our rooms with passing pleasures
but allowing the ark of our heart to be filled
with the fullness of life.

Mary's womb became the ark of the new covenant.
She is the singer and the song,
for her life reflects this attitude of trust
that God's promises to her would be fulfilled.
"Blessed are you among women," Elizabeth sings.
Blessed are we among all people when we realize
God desires to dwell among us.
God desires to play this song of joy in our lives.

This station on the way to the manger
invites us to clear the ark of our hearts
so that we can hear this music of God.
In the lyrics of our own lives,
we learn to listen in between the notes of this song
and find the true measure and meaning of joy.

I heard this song as I gazed upon the face of Annette.
It is a song that will linger in my soul for a long time,
so long as I give the song enough room, enough silence,
to play in the ark of my heart.

ECHOES OF MARY'S SONG

Such is the joy that God yearns for each of us to own.
We've known this joy, haven't we?
As we inch ever closer to the manger and beyond,
our spirits are lifted by small signs of hope and joy.
We put up the Christmas lights
and string some on the barren branches of trees.
In the darkest time of the year
they glow with the news that God is near.

By echoing Mary's song,
this station seeks to increase our capacity for joy.

The quality of joy at this way station is reflective and quiet.
It is the gentle silence etched in the smiles of two friends
sharing a meal after they haven't seen each other for a while.
Or it's the peaceful presence of a family gathering
in front of the fireplace on a cold winter's night,
keeping each other warm.

You know that phrase, "happy-go-lucky"?
I think it's true: the happy do go through life lucky.
Ah, but the joyful-go-graceful —
they go through life knowing they are like Mary,
full of grace.

At this station on the way to the manger
we spend some time getting to know that joy again.
We spend some time by the fire in the silence of prayer
or in the company of a good friend.
We slow the pace just a bit and give a glance or a good long gaze
at the face of someone we love,
someone in whom we recognize God's redeeming grace.

Just one thing, though:
When we come to know this joy deep in our hearts,
Let's be sure to notify our faces.

Fourth Station Prayer

We adore you, O Christ, and we bless you,
because by your holy birth you give hope to the world.

God of joy and laughter,
you have given me a song to sing with my life.
If I do not give voice to this song,
your music of love is muted.

Give me the courage to stand on the world's stage
and sing of the joy I hold not only deep in my heart
but in my body and soul.
May others see the lyrics of this song of joy
written on my face,
may they dance to the beat of its music,
and clap their hands in joyful praise.

O Loving God,
may a gentle smile always crease my soul
and cross my heart
so that when others hear
the sound of music singing in my life
it may ring in their hearts.

May my song of joy,
written by your creative hand,
magnify your greatness.
May my song of joy echo in all I am
and in all I do.

+*Amen.*

Fifth Station

Promulgation

FINDING OUR VOICE

And they made signs to his father,
inquiring what he would have him called.
And he asked for a writing tablet and wrote,
"His name is John."
Luke 1: 62-63

When the time came for the child born in his old age
to be presented to God,
Zechariah, who was dumbfounded initially by the news,
found his voice by claiming that his son would be called John.
His tongue was free again
because of his silent trust in the truth the angel spoke to him.

As the people began motioning to Zechariah
"to find out what name he wanted to give" the child,
I can imagine Zechariah's face, in Luke's descriptive phrase,
"go keen till the walls of the world flared, widened,"
and he wrote on the tablet, "His name is John."

Zechariah plays a supporting but important role in salvation's story.
In the prayer of the Church, the Liturgy of the Hours,
we honor Zechariah's memory each morning.
His canticle, the prayer he prays when he finds his voice,
becomes our morning prayer.

When Zechariah finds his voice,
he shows us what happens when the mountains
we seek to level are too steep to climb,
when the valleys where the shadows of death linger are too deep,
and when our trust in the possibility of miracles begins to wane.

Zechariah's story suggests to us that we are to hold fast to the hope
that God knows what God is doing.
This Fifth Station invites us to trust that God is calling forth from us
even in our tired and deadly routine
new ways of living the dream God holds for each of us.

We find our voice the same way Zechariah did:
We become mute before the awesome presence of God's promise.
We close our mouths, open our ears,
and go deeper into the mystery.

This station on the way to the manger
advises us to find that silent space within our own souls,
within the schedule of our busy days and restless nights,
to dwell in this divine mystery that human words cannot convey.
In our time in prayer, in silence,
we seek to create some space for God's Word
that will be spoken as our Advent anticipation
gives way to our Christmas celebration.

Finding our Advent voice means that first
we open our Advent ears in prayer
and listen once again to the Source.

THE PRAYER OF SILENCE

The angel of God touched Zechariah
from that mysterious place where God's Word is first formed.
Prayer is the way we try to connect with our Divine Source.
When we pray, we try to clear our minds and open our hearts
so the energy of God's spirit can course through us.

Prayer purifies our motivations,
clarifies our commitments
and clears the lines of communication
so that our lives might reflect the reality
of God's reign among us.

His eloquent silence purified Zechariah to trust
that God's word to him would be fulfilled.
In the silence of this station,
we wait and see, listen and learn,
as we seek to purify our hearts.
These days of silent waiting allow us to hear the voice of God
singing love songs in the chambers of our hearts,
for this is the chamber music that plays
the songs we hum in our souls.

When it came time for the child born in his old age
to be presented to God,
Zechariah found his voice when he motioned for a writing tablet,
and he had the last word by confirming his wife's decision
that their son should be called John.
Because of this promulgation,
his tongue was free again
and the first words that flowed from Zechariah's mouth
were words of praise to God.

The Word Made Flesh

In his silence, Zechariah trusted in the truth the angel spoke to him
that God's promises "will all come true in due season."

This is the season when God's promises come due.
On Christmas Day, the promises are paid in full.
According to the Letter to the Hebrews,
"Long ago, God spoke to our ancestors
in many and various ways by the prophets,
but in these last days God has spoken to us by a Son."
This season of hope celebrates how the Word of God
was made flesh in the person of Jesus Christ.

No longer does God speak to us with a muted voice
or in phrases we cannot understand.
With the birth of Jesus, God speaks with a human voice.
Oh, God still speaks to us in the beauty of creation
and the wonders of the universe,
in a gentle rain or a driving wind.
But now God's voice is unmistakable and clear.
God speaks our language.

This is the language we most need to hear
when our lives become a tangled mess of lies.
When relationships fail, we insult a friend,
we can't stand our job, our health turns sour,
this is the Word we hear in our silence.
God places the divine Word in a human voice,
and the message is clear: No matter what happens,
"I am with you always until the end of the world."

We don't start out in life wanting to make a mess.
Sometimes, however, despite our best efforts,

our lives become a mess.
But remember:
The Word is spoken first in a mess of a manger.
God sent the Son as the **mess**enger, the **Mess**iah,
to give us the **mess**age: Keep doing good.
Don't worry if you fail: just keep trying.

When life gets messy,
Jesus is born into the world to redeem the mess.
God's word is spoken here, and that word is redemption.

ANOTHER WORD FROM OUR SPONSOR

But there is another word spoken here.
It's a word from our sponsor
that is captured in a story
about the famous son of a famous father.
Though he won numerous awards for his writing,
Ring Lardner, Jr.'s, greatest claim to fame
was being blacklisted and branded a communist
in the infamous McCarthy hearings.

After winning an Academy Award in the early 1950s,
he didn't work for almost two decades because of his refusal
to cooperate with the House Un-American Activities Committee.
When he finally did win acceptance again in Hollywood,
he won another Academy Award for co-writing
the screenplay for the film M*A*S*H.

The story goes that many years after being blacklisted
he and his wife were attending a movie
when they ran into the man
who had turned Lardner's name into the House Committee.

This was the man who forced him
to be out of work for almost twenty years.
Lardner's wife turned away from the man,
but Lardner extended his hand.
When his wife asked him why he would extend a hand
to the man who betrayed him, he said,
"Because I don't believe in blacklisting."

God's Word is spoken here, and that word is reconciliation.

The Word of God came to earth to speak our language
so that we might learn a new language of unconditional love.
We know how difficult it is to learn this language.
Just as Zechariah found it difficult to believe
that God's promises would come due,
we know how difficult it is to put our hearts and minds and mouths
around that one word: love.

But as we seek to find our voice,
remember how God kept the divine promise
and how, when God's promise came due,
Zechariah found his voice.

And so will we.
The Word of God became flesh and lived among us.
The Word of God is spoken here,
and that Word is simple and sacred and so easy to pronounce:
God is with us.

God is always with us.
In the stress and the mess,
the hurry and the worry of this season,
and every other season,
the sign of Emmanuel means that God is with us.

God never leaves us.
We say it at the beginning
and end of every Eucharist and often in between:
"God is with you."
This is the greeting and the grace
that sustains and gives strength.
It is the sign of Emmanuel: God is with us.

As the clock winds down and the pace increases,
embrace the grace of the sign of this season.
When writing or receiving a Christmas card,
reflect on how that person or friend or family member
brought home the truth
that God is with us.
In all the preparations for this season, ask:
How am I reflecting the grace of Emmanuel?

This is the single sight that all the holly and hurry,
the wrapping paper and ribbons and worry,
the tinsel in the trees and lights on the houses,
the candles and the cards and the carols
are supposed to reflect:
God is with us.

Now isn't that better than God
choosing to be somewhere else?

Fifth Station Prayer

We adore you, O Christ, and we bless you,
because by your holy birth you give hope to the world.

At this station, O God,
a hush hovers over my heart
as I listen for the sound of your voice.
On a sleepless, still and silent night,
you spoke the Word
that brought Love into the world.

Open my ears that I may hear this Word.
For I will never find my voice
unless I first listen to your voice.
During the rush hours of my busy life,
allow me to find a few minutes of silence each day.
May this hush of prayer prepare me
to handle the rush of all the activities.
Create in me an inward calm to listen first
and only then to speak my truth.

Only when I listen for your Word
will I be able to sit with the worried
or weary or weak or wounded
as we wait to hear "good news."
And when we hear it,
give us the courage to find our voices
and to proclaim it with our lives.

+Amen.

Sixth Station

Declaration

SLEEPLESS IN NAZARETH

*Her husband Joseph, being a just man
and unwilling to put her to shame,
resolved to divorce her quietly.
But as he considered this, behold an angel of the Lord
appeared to him in a dream, saying,
"Joseph, son of David, do not fear to take Mary as your wife...."*
Matthew 1: 19-20

A few years ago, Tom Hanks and Meg Ryan
starred in a movie called *Sleepless in Seattle*.
It was about a couple who carried on a long-distance romance
via the telephone until they finally met in person.
A few years later, these same two actors reunited in the film
You've Got Mail.
This time they fall in love by exchanging email in cyberspace.

If a film were made about this Sixth Station,
Tom Hanks and Meg Ryan might be the perfect couple

to cast as Joseph and Mary.
We could call it *Sleepless in Nazareth*.
Except in this movie,
instead of coming together through cyberspace,
Mary and Joseph are reunited through sacred space
and the most ancient form of communication:
The voice of an angel.

Sleepless in Nazareth
opens with Joseph tossing and turning.
He can't sleep because he is in quite a quandary.
The woman he loves seems to have betrayed him.
Mary is pregnant, and Joseph knows he is not the father.
He has two choices:
expose his beloved to the law, which carries with it the death penalty,
or get rid of her quietly.
Either way, he loses the one he loves.
No wonder Joseph can't sleep.

When he is able to close his eyes and fall into a shallow sleep,
he has the wildest dream.
An angel appears and gives him a third option.

IN YOUR WILDEST DREAMS

In this wildest of dreams, the angel says it's okay to take Mary as his wife.
Mary has not been unfaithful to him; she has been faithful to God.
Something extraordinary has happened.
The child Mary carries in her womb was conceived by the Holy Spirit.
Then, or so the Gospel goes, "Joseph awoke from sleep."

That line might be this station's refrain.
The waiting and watching are nearing an end;
the hiding and hibernation are almost complete.

Soon we will awake to the dawn of a new day:
the birth of Christ.
Joseph's sleepless night, his wildest dream,
creeps across our consciousness to ask:
Are we awake?
Or are we still asleep?

Perhaps an even better script would ask:
Are we still "sleep running" through this busy time of year?
After all, none of us walks in our sleep in the weeks before Christmas.
There is too much to do. Everyone seems to be on the run.

When Joseph awoke, he showed us
the only kind of running worth our effort at this time of year.
As someone once said,
"There are times in life when one has to rush off in pursuit of hopefulness."
That is what Joseph did when he awoke:
He rushed off in pursuit of hopefulness and "took Mary as his wife."

But before he went to sleep that night,
Joseph had to be grieving.
Imagine the anguish in his heart.
Here is the woman with whom he intended to spend the rest of his life,
and now his future was crumbling around him.
The woman he was going to marry was carrying someone else's child.
How could this be happening to him? How could this be?"

Remember, that is the same question
Mary asked the angel at an earlier station:
"*How can this be,* since I do not know man?"
This angel, a most important supporting character
in this sacred script, this way to the manger,
reflects how God brings people together
in the sacred space of our dreams.

The angel's appearance in his wildest dream
gave Joseph the courage to remain faithful to Mary.
Though he could not comprehend it,
Joseph took the angel's words to heart.
When he awoke from his dream,
he rushed off in pursuit of hopefulness.

WAKING UP A DREAM

Now, it's one thing to dream and quite another to act on one's dream.
And that's what Joseph did.
He allowed his dream to guide his every step, his every action.
Because Joseph believed in the power of his dream,
he fashioned a future with Mary.
Though he certainly did not understand the full implications of the dream
or how the dream would be played out,
he humbly accepted his role in God's surprising salvation story.

Joseph stayed awake.
He followed the angel's counsel and took Mary into his care.
I wonder what Joseph said to Mary when they met
the first time after he had this dream?
I'm sure a Hollywood scriptwriter could come up with
just the right dialogue.
But for my money, I suspect there was silence.
A wordless embrace,
a holy silence,
that spoke of a love so rare and so wonderful.
We can picture the scene:
Mary and Joseph holding on to each other for dear life,
and for a dream so much larger than either one of them could conceive.

Yes, a silence that spoke of a love
that is stronger than fear, rejection, ambiguity, even betrayal.

A love that is stronger than death.
It's the kind of love that this child Mary carried in her womb
would attempt to make less rare.
Because Joseph trusted his dream,
we see how this kind of love is possible.

Dare we believe that God is dreaming in us again?
Dare we believe in new dreams of peace and reconciliation?
Dare we hold fast to God's dreams for us,
holding them tenderly yet tenaciously?
Dare we trust that in the womb of our dreams
hope is waiting to be born?

Joseph was such a daring dreamer.
At this Sixth Station, we remember that in the rush of our lives
true love rushes in where reason fears to tread.
This station teaches us to learn more
about daring dreams that make true love less rare.
Like Joseph, the sleep-deprived carpenter from Nazareth,
we trust God's wildest dreams for us
and pursue the only Christmas rush that holds any meaning:
the rush to hopefulness.

A FISH STORY

Dreams do come true — and not just in the movies.
But for our faith to make a difference,
dreams planted while we are asleep must come to life while we are awake.
Our dreams are to be lived out in real situations by real people.
Mary and Joseph were real people.
The characters in the following story are not real
but their names have been changed anyway,
in order, as they say in Hollywood, to protect the innocent.

"This is how the birth of Frankie Fish came about.
When his mother, Wanda Walleye, was engaged to Tom Tuna
but before they were married, she became pregnant."
Sound familiar?
Wanda Walleye and Tom Tuna were a very devout couple.
They went to church on Sunday, singing in the choir at 10 o'clock Mass
and both taught in the religious education program on Wednesday nights.
Wanda and Tom were a dream couple
that any pastor would love to have in his parish.
Indeed, Fr. Mackerel, their pastor, who was called "holy" by some,
certainly did appreciate their contributions to the parish
and met with them regularly for pre-Cana instructions.

But a few weeks before the wedding,
Wanda told Tom the stunning news that she was pregnant.
Tom knew he could not be the father and was shattered.
Wanda tried to explain to him that it was by the Holy Spirit
that she had conceived this child.
"Right," Tom said.
"It's true," Wanda said. "Trust me."

But Tom didn't buy it.
In fact, he was worried that Wanda was having delusions
and was in need of some psychiatric care.
Though he loved her deeply,
he could not possibly go through with the wedding.
When asked his opinion about the matter,
Fr. Mackerel said with a sigh, "It sounds fishy to me."

Trust Me

Joseph didn't buy it either.
He was ready to divorce Mary — he had to, because they were engaged,

and under the law, betrothal was as permanent a commitment as
marriage itself.
But he still loved Mary and didn't want to "expose her to the law"
and the shame and scorn and maybe even stoning that might ensue,
so he decided to divorce her quietly.
That's when the angel got in the way to save the day.

By paying attention to his dreams, Joseph found the courage to go on.
He found the ability to trust that God
was doing something extraordinary here.
As he continued to let go of his fear and feelings of betrayal,
he was able to see that Mary had not been unfaithful and that
what she had told him was true — she was bearing God's child.

Because Joseph believed in the power of his dream,
he fashioned a future with Mary,
and though he certainly did not understand
the full implications of the dream or how the dream would be played out,
he humbly accepted his role in God's surprising plan of salvation.

This is not a fish story but a faith story.
It says: Trust God even when our dreams turn to dust
and the odds are stacked against us.
Trust in the surprises that God has in store for us.
Trust in the light that glows within,
even when the darkness tempts us with its tendency to overcome the light.
Trust in God's dream for us and our world,
even when the nightmares of war and oppression
and famine and fear fail to take a holiday.
Like Joseph, we are to hold fast to God's dream for us —
tenaciously and yet tenderly.
We are to trust that in the womb of our dreams
hope is waiting to be born.

Sixth Station Prayer

We adore you, O Christ, and we bless you,
because by your holy birth you give hope to the world.

When I am restless and cannot sleep, O God,
I don't want to count sheep.
I want to count on you.

When I fall asleep too easily,
shake my slumber with dreams that startle me to see
that the abundant gifts you have given me
are not saved for a snowy day
but are to be given away.

Like your servant Joseph,
may I always be open to the surprise awareness
that of all your attributes
surprise is at the top of the list.
So it's important that we get to the bottom of things.
By paying attention and trusting the dreams
you have planted in my soul,
I will be prepared for whatever might happen
or whoever might cross my path this day.

+Amen.

Nativity

A Barn in Bethlehem County

And she gave birth to her firstborn son
and wrapped him in swaddling clothes,
and laid him in a manger,
because there was no place for them in the inn.
Luke 2: 7

There are many sounds we associate with this time of year.
We hear sleigh bells and silver bells,
bells rung by Salvation Army Santas
and church bells that peel away the night.
We hear the sounds of horns honking in parking lots
as desperate drivers seek the last available space
within shouting distance of the shopping mall,
and sounds of singers blowing dust off familiar Christmas carols.
But there is one sound we probably don't identify
with these sounds of this season.
It is the sound that brings more than a measure of meaning

to all the other sounds we hear at this time of year.
It is the sound we find in this story:

The little town of Bethlehem was bustling and busting at the seams
that night so many years ago.
Though the traditional Christmas carol we sing
conveys a sense of stillness and quiet sleep
hovering over this small town five miles south of Jerusalem,
that picture must have been taken well after midnight
because earlier in the evening, the streets were crowded.
The folks who flooded the streets of the little town of Bethlehem
were not frantic, last-minute shoppers in search of a gift certificate
from Sarah's Big and Tall Sweater Shop
or Benjamin and Jeremiah's Ice Cream Parlor.
The people who crowded into the tiny town of Bethlehem
were from various places; they had come to their hometown
to register for the census.

So, the houses were full of long-lost relatives who years before
had escaped the confines of the tiny town of Bethlehem
for the bright lights of the big city of Jerusalem.
The hotels and motels were overbooked.
Of course, there were not many places for travelers to lodge anyway,
because Bethlehem was always known as a place
where people came *from* and rarely went *to* or even *through*.
So, the "no vacancy" signs were everywhere:
on houses of relatives and houses of prayer,
on motels and hotels.
There was just no room in Bethlehem.

Into such a crowded place as this walked a young couple
who had made the long journey from the north to fulfill their patriotic duty.
Since Nazareth was in Galilee, many miles north of Jerusalem,

it had been an exhausting trip.
The young man hadn't been to his hometown since he was a child.
His mother and father moved to Nazareth when he was
four or five years old.
Bethlehem was so small that there just wasn't enough building going on
in the town to support his father's small construction company.
As they walked through the busy streets that night,
the young man looked at the faces in the crowd,
hoping that by luck or by chance or even by a casual glance
he might recognize the features of a distant cousin
or a long forgotten childhood friend
who might provide a place for his wife and him to stay
while they were in town.
But all the faces were unfamiliar.
When the third innkeeper he tried refused them a room,
the young man knew the time was growing short.
This was not a deadline he had to meet, but a lifeline:
His wife was pregnant and was due to give birth very soon.
He had to find a safe place where she could rest.
She'd been riding for several days and was in great pain.
When he looked into her eyes after coming out of the inn,
his wife's eyes told him: "It's time."

No Vacancy

The sound of the innkeeper nailing the "no vacancy" sign
to the door of his motel sparked a memory in the young man.
The sound of the hammer pounding reminded him
that the last building his father built when they still lived in Bethlehem
was a barn on a farm just outside of town.
He was only a boy at the time,
but he went with his father every day to that building site

to hand him nails or hold a board in place while his father hammered.
Though the young man had some doubts that the barn
would still be standing,
he decided it was their only chance.
Through the crowded streets of that tiny town of Bethlehem,
the young man led his wife.

Though he didn't trust his memory,
he trusted his instincts and found the barn.
It was still standing, a sign, he thought,
of his father's competent carpentry.
When he opened the door of the barn,
the smell of manure was overwhelming.
But there was no more time. This would have to do.
Into this smelly barn his father had built so many years before,
into this barn in Bethlehem County which was as crowded
as the streets of the tiny town —
crowded not with people but with cows and chickens and an ox —
the young man brought his pregnant wife.
He piled up some hay and straw in the corner of the barn,
helped his wife off the mule and carried her to the place he had prepared.
And there, in that barn, the time arrived.
His wife gave birth to a son.

Late that night,
after the young man watched his baby boy fall asleep in his wife's arms,
weary from the long journey and the even longer night,
the young man closed his eyes.
No sooner than he began to sleep did he have a dream.
In the dream, he saw himself standing on a hill
not far from the barn where he now slept.
He saw workers tearing down the barn that his father had built so long ago.

As the boards of the barn were tossed on a wagon,
the young man walked up to one of the workers and asked,
"Where are you taking the wood of this barn that my father built,
the wood of this barn where my son was born?"

"We are taking the wood to Jerusalem," the worker replied.
"But this wood is so old," the young man said.
"Certainly it won't be used in building homes or even another barn.
What kind of construction project
could use such remnant pieces of wood?"

"It will be used by the emperor."

"The emperor?
What possible use could the emperor have for such old wood?"

The worker looked at the young man and said,
"The emperor needs this aged wood to carry out
the decree of capital punishment.
You see, he decided not to waste good wood on criminals
who are crucified.
This old wood will be used to construct new crosses
for those sentenced to die."

The young man woke from his dream
with a pounding in his chest and his head.
The sound of a hammer driving nails into wood
kept him awake the rest of the night.
As he looked at the child asleep in his mother's arms,
he wished that sound reminded him of the day his father had built the barn.
But he knew that sound was meant for his son.

A DANGEROUS MEMORY

At that moment, or so it seemed for the young man and his wife,

time stood still in that barn in Bethlehem County.
For the birth of this child marks time: BC and AD.
From that crowded barn
just outside the tiny town of Bethlehem,
this child's reach would stretch across miles and memories,
to challenge the boundaries of who we are
and what we can do.

Into our crowded lives where there is no room,
a child is born.
At this Seventh Station, we take our own census
and return to those sacred places
and holy spaces in our lives where our faith was born.
Like that young man and his pregnant wife,
we walk through the streets of our crowded minds and hearts.
We see the faces of family members
and try to remember the names of long-forgotten friends.

We trace the genealogy of God's grace
that has appeared in our lives through the years.
We read the names and see the faces of those who,
by their teaching and their temperament, taught us
to "act justly, love tenderly and walk humbly with our God."

This is the station where we touch again the faces
of our mothers and fathers,
grandfathers and grandmothers,
sisters and brothers, aunts and uncles,
cousins and classmates and childhood friends,
playmates and prayer-mates, teachers and mentors,
lovers and spouses, children and companions,
and give thanks for the light that shone through them
and showed us the way.

This is not a mindless stroll down memory lane
but a mindful one.
We are mindful of those people who meant so much to us
and those who are so important to us today
because they help us tap into and touch again the goodness within
that so often gets lost in the busyness of making a living,
or making a life, or making it on our own.
We are mindful of the dreams we dared to share with them,
and we make room in our crowded memories for gratitude
for who they are and will be again as we long to be together.

At this way station, we visit in our minds and hearts
our old hometown that we left behind long ago.
We go back home to the places and the people with whom we belong.
We see the tree we used to climb, the room where we used to sleep,
the backyard where we played when the days seemed to be longer.
We remember the smells of our mother's kitchen
on a Sunday morning after church.
We remember the table and listen again to the talk
that seemed so unimportant and yet held us together.

This is the station where certain carols evoke special memories,
where certain sights provoke powerful recollections,
where certain sounds —
like a hammer nailing a "no vacancy" sign to a door —
produce the place where hope can be born.

But as dreamlike and delightful as this stroll down the crowded main street
of our own little towns of Bethlehem may be, it is also dangerous.
For this is also the time when we seem to remember
what we would like to forget:
those broken spaces, those distant places in our relationships,
those faces we vowed never to see or speak to again.

This Seventh Station captures how a child is given to us
to redeem those shattered spaces, bring closer those distant places
and restore those tear-stained faces to their youthful glow.

For this child who is given to us
is no longer confined in the womb of his mother
but is now let loose upon the world.
This child cries for our attention and affection.
This child demands our time and our trust.
This child beckons us to believe
that everyone and everything in our own little worlds
now revolve around him
so that anything or anyone
who is broken or distant or unforgiven
now can begin again.

Yes, into our crowded little minds and hearts,
full of jagged edges and sharp memories
that still cause us to hurt and to bleed,
comes a child who seeks only to heal
and give hope.

Seventh Station Prayer

We adore you, O Christ, and we bless you,
because by your holy birth you give hope to the world.

Loving God,
at this station you help me slip into something more comfortable:
the swaddling clothes of my dependence upon you.
These swaddling clothes seem very uncomfortable at first.
But then, they are cut from the cloth with the union label that reads,
"the last shall be first."
This is the only label that can fashion our unity.

Wrapped in these swaddling clothes,
I come to know that I am not in control.
And only when I know that I am not in control
will I come to know true freedom
and enjoy being a child again.

I'm tired of trying to save face, O God.
So help me to see your face in the eyes of my beloved,
in the smile of a friend,
in the frown of a coworker,
in the wrinkled wisdom lines of a parent,
in the smooth features of a child,
in the stare of a stranger,
in the blemished beauty of a forgotten love.

Into the streets of my little town, O God,
you come looking for a place to lay your head.
Lay your head upon my heart,
make yourself comfortable.
Make yourself at home.

+*Amen.*

Eighth Station

Observation

And in that region there were shepherds out in the field,
keeping watching over their flock by night.
An angel appeared to them,
and the glory of the Lord shone around them,
and they were filled with fear.
Luke 2: 8-9

When I moved to a farm in southern Illinois in the fall of 1998,
it was the first time I ever lived near sheep.
Shepherds play an important part in the story of Christ's birth,
and Jesus often used sheep in his storytelling.
He identified himself as the Good Shepherd,
who would be willing to leave the ninety-nine sheep in the fold
in search of the one that got away.

The affinity Jesus shows for shepherds and sheep —
as opposed to, say, goats, who certainly get the sharp end of the stick
in the final judgment scene in Matthew 25 —
raises the question of what they have to teach us about hope.

Shepherds are very protective of their flock.
They don't want to lose even one sheep.
If they see that one has gone astray,
in the pattern of the parable of the Good Shepherd,
they will focus all of their energy on the one that got away.

When I lose something that is very important to me,
I search high and low trying to find it.
I retrace my steps and try to remember
the last time I saw this precious possession.
I might even call someone to come and help me look.
I will not give up the search until I have found what I have lost.

But when I have lost something that is not very important to me,
I give up the search rather quickly.
I might say to the friend who is helping me look,
"Well, it will turn up," and go on about my business.

In the lost-and-found department of our lives,
our desire to find what is lost is based on how important
that possession — or that person — is to us.
We will expend all our energy and time
in looking for what has been lost,
whether it is a family heirloom or a friend.

As seekers of hope,
this Eighth Station underscores the extraordinary concern God has for us,
especially those among us who are feeling lost or forsaken.
God is willing to go to the absolute limits,
beyond a reasonable search, to find us.
We are the lost, and God came to earth to find us.
Now you might argue that when the shepherds keeping watch
over their flock that night saw the light of the angel
and left their post in search of the child,

they were not being "good shepherds"
because they left their flocks unprotected.
Or maybe they were leaving the ninety-nine
in search of the Paschal Lamb,
the one who will identify so closely with the "one that got away."

We will have a difficult time understanding
this unreasonable search of the shepherds
if we have not experienced the extravagant love of God.
In terms of percentages,
ninety-nine out of a hundred sheep is not at all a bad score.
If we think in these terms,
then we will never understand the kind of rejoicing that took place
when the shepherds arrived at the manger and saw the child
who will be called "the Lamb of God."
Nor will we understand the joy in heaven when the lost sheep is found.

But if we have experienced reconciliation
with someone in our lives who has been lost for a while,
we can understand such joy.
At this station,
take an inventory of the people in your life who are lost —
the people who, for whatever reason,
seem distant and far from the table of your love.
Focus all of your energy and prayer on those who are lost.
It might be an old friend with whom you've had a disagreement
that has caused some distance.
It may be someone in your family who is going through a difficult time
and is sitting on the sharp edge of despair.
It may be someone at work or in the neighborhood
who is feeling disconnected or discouraged.
In your prayer today, lift them up on your shoulders
and trust that God will find them even if you have lost them.

Remember that the reason for our hope
is that God came to earth to find what was lost.

HOPE: SCANNING THE SKIES

Grace is the light
that shines through the windows of our souls
into the nooks and crannies of our lives
to find what is lost in our lives
and to sweep out the darkness of sin and death.

This light streams into our lives
to wash the floors clean with the mercy of our God.
But this is more than a stream of mercy,
it is a flood of forgiveness that not only washes the floor,
it knocks down the doors and tears down the walls
of our resistance to God's love.

This floodlight of God's forgiving love
that streaks across the night sky and falls to earth
catches the attention of a few "shepherds living in the fields,
keeping watch over their flock by night."

These shepherds are the anonymous figures of the Christmas story.
In the first part of the story,
we hear all kinds of names and places to set the scene:
Mary and Joseph, Herod and Caesar, Nazareth and Bethlehem.

But these shepherds are out in a field,
nameless, faceless folk who become the first to see the light.
An "angel of God stood before them,
and the glory of God shone around them."
These shepherds were scared to death,
but the angel of light gave them a birth announcement:

"Do not be afraid...this day in the city of David
a Savior is born to you."

These shepherds, of course,
symbolize the poor and lowly, the outcasts and aliens,
the foreigners and fringe people of society.
But this group was not the tenderhearted image
we associate with Jesus when he calls himself the "Good Shepherd."
These were tough guys.
Sure, they would go out looking for lost sheep,
but they would do so armed with clubs
just in case they might encounter a poacher or a predator.
The Pharisees and religious leaders thought shepherds were unclean,
so they were not allowed in the synagogue.
Others saw them as rustic and irresponsible.
These shepherds were down-to-earth, gritty characters,
who rolled up their sleeves to work and fight hard.
They were not accustomed to falling to their knees for anyone.
But I suspect they had never seen a choir of angels
belting out the alleluia chorus before.

To such as these, the floodlights of God's forgiveness flash first.
It is not surprising that Luke gives the shepherds such a prominent place
in the Christmas story as the first ones who see the light.
They are the working poor,
scraping by from paycheck to paycheck, working the graveyard shift.
To these shepherds the angel gives a sign:
"You will find a child wrapped in swaddling clothes
and lying in a manger."
To find this child,
they need only follow a star that will serve as a searchlight.

This is the same searchlight that helps those

who have trouble finding room at an inn or a place at the table
to find rest for their soul.
This is the light we see in our children's eyes
when they open their presents and say,
"It's just what I wanted!"
It is the light we have all known
and will know again if we are willing
to look deeply into the eyes of those we love
and those we find difficult to love.
For it is a light that illuminates and illustrates
the enormous opportunities we have to heal the brokenhearted,
to set captives free,
to find the lost and feed the hungry,
to reconnect with those who, for whatever reason, are distant
and to practice reconciliation in all our relationships.

This light embraces us because "the grace of God has appeared."
If we have grown tired and weary from giving our best
and receiving little in return,
then this is the station to let the light of hope shine through.
The grace of God has appeared.

If we have forsaken opportunities to pray
or to pursue peace or to make justice more real in our day
because of fear, this is the station to let the light give us courage.
In the angels' words to the shepherds, "Do not be afraid."
The grace of God has appeared.

If there is someone we have left outside the door of our understanding,
someone who has been standing at the window
longing to be warmed by the fire of our love,
this is the station to let the light of forgiveness shine in.
The grace of God has appeared.

Like those shepherds who were the first to see this light
cascading down from the sky on the wings of angels,
I wonder: In what relationship,
in what place of my life
do I need to see this light?

If we dwell in darkness,
this Eighth Station provides more than enough light.
If our heartland is filled with gloom or doom or despair,
at this station we can embrace a new light.

Especially for those on the fringes of our lives,
those we had pushed away or believed had gone astray,
this is the station where shepherds observe in the night sky
a searchlight that seeks them out and shows them the way home.

For at this station we hear,
"a child is born to us, a son is given us."
We name this child
"Wonder-Counselor,
God-Hero,
Father-Forever,
Prince of Peace."
This light is a flood of forgiveness
that washes away our resentments and our fears.
This light is a stream of mercy that need not be measured
but can be poured out without fear or favor to others.
This light bathes us with glory and beckons us to believe again
that with this light shining within us,
a new day has dawned.

Eighth Station Prayer

We adore you, O Christ, and we bless you,
because by your holy birth you give hope to the world.

Gracious God,
you are the Good Shepherd,
always on the lookout for the one that got away.
When I feel small because my love is not large,
you come looking for me in my hiding place
and provide me with a safe place,
not so I can lick my wounds
but so that you can heal them.

When I am bruised and battered by the events of my life,
you comfort me with your tender compassion.
When I am stubborn and so sure of myself,
you show me the path of humility and hope.
When I am at my lowest, you raise me up.

Forgiving God, help me always to remember
that when I feel like the greatest sinner
I become a candidate for your widest mercy.
When I am disgraced and disgusted with myself,
you send a stream of redeeming grace to wash me clean
and a gust of wind to blow my sin away.

Lamb of God,
teach me to be always on the lookout —
to seek out the lost,
to welcome the stranger,
to clothe the naked
and to announce with my life
the favor of your forgiving love.

+Amen.

Ninth Station

Nomination

SANTA'S STOCKING STUFFER

At the end of eight days, when he was circumcised,
he was called Jesus, the name given by the angel
before he was conceived in the womb.
Luke 2: 21

The first and most precious gift we receive is the gift of life.
But soon after we are born, we are given a gift that most of us
take with us the rest of our lives.
It is the gift of our name.
At this Ninth Station we celebrate our nomination as children of God
who are named for the One who walks this way of life and hope with us.

Every year for as long as I can remember
there has been a gift under the Christmas tree with my name on it
that I don't have to shake to figure out what's inside.
When I see the card "From Santa, to Joe,"
I know what's inside the box: socks.

Now, I admit, socks are better than coal!
For the three years I lived in a cabin in the woods
and had to walk through rain and snow and mud
to get to the house of prayer where I worked,
I actually asked Santa for socks —
preferably wool socks to keep my feet warm and dry
when I walked through the woods.

But before that I couldn't figure out why Santa
would give me socks for Christmas.
I received other gifts from Mom and Dad and family members,
but the gift from Santa was always the same thing: socks.

Then one year,
with the help of G.K. Chesterton, I finally figured it out.
The British author writes about how, as a child,
he was "faced with a phenomenon requiring explanation."
Before he went to bed on Christmas Eve,
he would hang an empty stocking at the foot of the bed —
an appropriate place to place a sock, wouldn't you say?
When he awoke on Christmas morning,
the empty sock would be filled with all kinds of treats and toys and candy.
"I did nothing to produce the things that filled the stocking,"
Chesterton wrote.
"I had not worked for them, or made them or helped to make them.
I had not even been good — far from it.
And the explanation was that a certain being
whom people called Santa Claus
was benevolently disposed toward me."

This was, for Chesterton, the meaning of Christmas:
that whether he was "naughty or nice"
the one who filled his stocking loved him unconditionally.

He didn't have to earn this love, nor did he have to work for it.
His stocking was stuffed with good things
simply because someone loved him.

FILLING THE SOCKS

As he grew older, Chesterton simply expanded
this idea about Santa's stuffing stockings.
"Once I thought it delightful and astonishing
to find a present so big that it only went halfway into the stocking.
Now I am delighted and astonished every morning to find a present so big
that it takes two stockings to hold it, and then leaves a great deal outside;
it is the large and preposterous present of myself."

This is why socks on Christmas are the perfect gift:
the celebration of the Incarnation underscores our belief that the One
who created the sun and moon and stars;
the One who created the mountains and hills,
the flowers and trees, the birds and the bees;
the One who created us
became one of us!
This God of ours slipped into our stocking feet
to walk among us as a human being.
God came to earth in the person of Jesus
to walk for miles and millenniums
in our shoes and socks or sandals or even bare feet.
We did nothing to deserve or to earn this great gift.
We did nothing to merit God's attention and affection.
But out of the greatness of God's generous heart,
God decided to come among us as a human being
and to show us how to live as a gift to one another.

When we place our feet into our socks or stockings,
we reflect God's greatest gift.

We are God's great gift to one another!
Life, family, friends, community,
all the people we have known and loved,
all the people who have touched our lives
with God's presence through the years —
we are the gifts that overflow our stocking feet!

WASHING MUDDY FEET

This one who is given the name Jesus
shows us how to walk in each other's shoes and socks for a while,
and so we begin to understand how each of us
is a gift from the gracious heart of God.

But we who receive this nomination and claim the name of Christ
know that following Christ is not as easy as following tracks in the snow.
If it was, we could look at the tracks that led us away from God
and see how we lost our way.
We could retrace our steps of infidelity and allow God to lead us home.
Still, at this Ninth Station we can check our bearings.
And even if there isn't a trace of snow on the ground,
we can still check our tracks.

We can do this by remembering how this One
who had received the nomination to be prince of peace
would, on the very night before he died,
get down on his knees and wash the feet of his disciples.
In this act of loving service,
he gave us an example of how we who bear his name
are to do the same:
to take off each others' shoes and socks and wash the feet of all.

Jesus got down on his knees to wash the feet of those on the run.
He knew they would run this night — they would run the other way.

But he washed their feet anyway —
even the feet of the one who would betray him.

"Do you understand what I have just done for you?"
he asked his disciples.
Jesus, the one whose nomination implies Teacher, Master, Lord,
was down on his knees.
This is where compassionate service done in his name begins and ends:
on our knees.

Remember how Peter missed the point of what Jesus was doing?
He put up a fuss about having his feet washed.
But Peter was on firm footing here.
It was unheard of that the One who had won the nomination —
the leader and teacher — should assume this position,
a posture of humility, even humiliation.
But Jesus had long ago assumed this position —
from the time of his birth and certainly from his baptism,
when his cousin John said he was unworthy to untie Jesus' sandals,
let alone baptize him: "It is you who should be baptizing me."

Peter was just following the standards set up before him.
That is why he was so insistent: "You shall never wash my feet!"
But upon learning the consequences of unwashed feet —
that he would be cut out of God's will
and have no share in Jesus' inheritance —
he scrambled to take off his sandals.
In fact, Peter wanted a pedicure and a shampoo too:
"Not only my feet but my hands and head as well!"

Several years ago I heard an interview with Michael Blake,
the author who wrote the screenplay for the film *Dances With Wolves*.
After years of trying to make it in Hollywood,
this author finally hit the big time.

He won an Academy Award for his work.
In his late 40s, only a few years before this break,
he was washing dishes in a restaurant to earn some money
since his screenplays had been rejected time and time again.

Now, he had it made. Or so he thought.
Shortly after earning a substantial amount of money and winning an Oscar,
he found out he had cancer.
In response to a question about his illness
coming right at the time of his greatest success, the writer said,
"A poet friend of mine told me not to worry about it.
It's just a reminder always to keep one foot in the mud."

On that night before his Teacher died,
Peter learned firsthand what it means to always keep one foot in the mud.
It was a primary reason why the One who won the nomination
had come to wash the feet of those who stand knee-deep
in the mud of their tears and their bloodcurdling fears.

No More Cold Feet

This is why socks are not only a practical
but a prophetic and sacred gift for Christmas.
On a winter's night in Bethlehem
the world's cold feet were warmed by the birth of a child.
Shepherds who were minding their own business
were startled by the light that shined upon them.
And what did the angel say to them?
"Do not be afraid."
Or, as another translation might have put it,
"Do not have cold feet!"

How important is this gift?
We can't speak out for justice and work for peace with cold feet.

If we have cold feet, we won't walk with those who are lonely
or lingering on the fringes of our society or our community of faith.
If we have cold feet, we won't take the risk
to get down on our knees and wash the feet of others.
If we have cold feet, we won't spread the good news;
we won't walk in another's shoes;
we won't proclaim with our lives
the favor of God's forgiveness, mercy and love
that God shows us with the nomination of the Son as savior.

What this station seeks to teach us, my warm-footed friends,
is how we are also nominated to be light and warmth and hope
to a world that has grown cold.
Our socks and stockings are stuffed not with things we don't really need
but with a God who knows our every need —
a God who becomes a human being
and shows us how to walk in the light of the child named Jesus.

So now I know why Santa gives me socks every year.
When we slip on a new pair of socks or stockings each day,
we become God's stocking stuffers.
We are God's gift to one another.
We are God's light to the world.

Socks are a sacred symbol.
And even if our socks are worn out from the wear and tear of walking,
even if we grow weary walking with one another
and washing each other's feet,
God knows firsthand what we need.
Because of God's stocking-stuffer gift of a Son, God knows what we suffer.
God knows our joy. God knows our pain.
For this child named Jesus walks with us every step of the way
and will show us the way home.

Ninth Station Prayer

We adore you, O Christ, and we bless you,
because by your holy birth you give hope to the world.

Warmhearted God,
I thank you for not having cold feet
when you decided to make the giant leap
to become human.

Though at times I give you a cold shoulder,
you never give up on me.
You are always there,
on your knees,
wanting to wash my cold feet.

Give me the courage, Brave-hearted God,
to wash the feet of others.
May I never be embarrassed by the holes in my socks
to take off my shoes and allow another
to extend that kindness to me.

At times pride gets the best of me,
and, like Peter, I announce boldly and emphatically,
"You will never wash my feet!"
Teach me to be humble in your service, O God.
As your Son taught us when he walked upon the earth,
it is only when we learn how to walk in another's sandals
that the scandal of our indifference to the plight of others
will take flight in our service to one another.

As I put on my socks and shoes this morning, O God,
may I see how I am your gift to all I will meet this day.

+ *Amen.*

Tenth Station

Manifestation

THOUGHTS THAT COUNT

When they saw the star, they rejoiced exceedingly with great joy;
and going into the house they saw the child with Mary his mother,
and they fell down and worshiped him.
Matthew 2: 10-11

Have you ever opened a gift on Christmas Day
and whispered to yourself,
"Well, it's the thought that counts"?
We usually reserve this phrase for a gift
that doesn't quite fit our person or personality.
I wonder if this thought crossed Mary's mind
as she saw the strange gifts of the Magi:
"It's the thought that counts."

When I hear that phrase, I wonder:
How much is a thought worth these days?
And if the thought counts more than the gift,
why not just give the thought?

What thoughts cross our minds at this station?
Hold those thoughts. Give them as gifts. They count.
I don't know how much because I'm not sure
in the age of inflation what the price is for thoughts.
I've heard of "thoughts weighing heavy on peoples' minds,"
but these thoughts do not make good gifts.
They are like that gift of myrrh
used in Jesus' time to prepare bodies for burial.
Now that's a heavy gift to give to a baby.

I'm not sure about this,
but it seems to me that the more thoughts weigh the less they count.
So it's good to lighten up.

Send only good thoughts at this Tenth Station.
This seems appropriate since I recall when growing up
that bad thoughts were often on my list for confession, not Christmas.
We wouldn't want to send bad thoughts anyway.
Often these are very heavy to carry.
Good thoughts are light as feathers.

I often write in many of my Christmas cards,
"You are in my thoughts and prayers."
I don't know why I make a distinction
between "thoughts" and "prayers."
After all, can't a thought be a prayer?
We might say in a moment of illumination,
"Hey, I just had a thought."
Could we also say in such moments,
"Hey, I just had a prayer."
We *say* prayers and *have* thoughts.
But when the thought is spoken
it no longer counts as a thought

because now the inspiration is out in the open.
It is an incarnation.
People hear it, maybe even see it,
judge it, embrace it or dismiss it.
It's only a thought. But now it counts.

On Second Thought

The point of all this is that if God only gave us a thought
or maybe even a prayer,
there would be no point to this pilgrimage.
We might say, "It's the thought that counts,"
but these stations celebrate how God's thought became a Word
and that "Word was made flesh."
The Word was spoken from the depth of God's heart
on a silent, starry night.
Indeed, this Word began as a Divine Thought —
a Word that holds all the hope,
all the love, all the compassion
in the Divine Heart.

Imagine with me, then, having a conversation with God
to thank God for this "Word made flesh."
And God says, "Don't give it a second thought."
These are the words we might say to brush off a gesture of gratitude.
God sees the look in our eyes.
God sees how we really want to express our thanks
for this greatest of gifts.
And God says, "You know, on second thought,
what you're thanking me for is the incarnation
of my second thoughts."

This surprises us.
Because when we say we're having "second thoughts,"

we mean we're having doubts about what we might do.
Having second thoughts implies a change of heart.
"You're not having second thoughts about coming to earth, are you, God?"

God laughs. "No," God says,
"My second thought offers you another chance
not to change your minds but to change your heart.
You see, my first thought was, 'Let there be light.'
These are the first words you attribute to me in the Scripture.
This was my first outburst as recorded in the book of Genesis.
These words express my very first thought at the beginning of creation.
'Let there be light.' And there was light.
You see, the thought, once expressed,
became an incarnation that resulted in oceans and stars, mountains and hills,
birds and plants, animals of every kind and of the human kind.

"But my first thought, this initial inspiration,
was rejected by the garden variety man and woman I created.
I had to banish these first two words that became flesh
from the garden of earthly delight.
It seems to me you've been trying to get back Eden ever since."

"So," we ask God,
"were you having second thoughts about creation at that point?"
God smiles.
"Oh, I've had many second thoughts
in between the Garden of Eden and the birth of Jesus.
The story of Noah and the great flood comes to mind.
I've also had great second thoughts
that include such notable, thought-provoking
patriarchs and prophets, matriarchs and messengers
as Abraham and Sarah, Moses and Miriam,
Joseph and Hannah, Isaiah and Ruth.

I bent an ear and lent a hand for centuries
to rescue the manifestations of my first thought.
Take, for example, when the people were in slavery in Egypt.

"But my greatest second thought," God says,
"was when I decided that instead of sending
prophets and poets, messengers and mystics
to try to change the hearts and minds of my people,
I would do something new.
I thought, 'Why don't I just go myself?'
On second thought,
I had an angel bring this divine idea to a peasant girl named Mary
who was engaged to be married to a carpenter named Joseph.
Mary's relative, Elizabeth, and her speechless husband —
the high priest who couldn't preach for a while
because this second thought stretched his heart
so far it strained his vocal chords — were also in the picture.
My second thought would bring the world to its knees
by lifting this maiden, this lowly one, to high places.

"And so, one night,
this divine inspiration, this second thought, became a Word.
I spoke this Word on a dark, clear night, when the stars were bright,
the town was crowded, and the shepherds were awake.
On this night, this second thought became very much like the first,
which manifested in the creation of the universe.
I said, 'Let there be a Light of the World.'
And that thought, once spoken in the silence of a holy night,
changed forever the course of history."

Easy for God to Say

So when we consider the gifts of the Magi
of gold, frankincense and myrrh,

remember that not only does the thought count,
but the Word counts even more.

This station reminds us that God's thought
has been turned into a Word,
and that Word became flesh and blood, bone and soul.
This word, we might say, is easy for God to say
because God is infinite, incomprehensible, divine.
But don't we see, can't we hear,
that it is because God saw how we were having
such difficulty understanding and translating God's first thought
that on second thought God made the divine Word human?
Spoken in the language all humankind can understand:
the language of love.
The love that is seen when a mother
holds her firstborn child close to her heart.
This is the scene the Magi saw after their long journey.
It is the magnificent manifestation of God's love to the world.
In this awe-filled moment, these men of majesty
saw the glory of God revealed.

It is also significant to recall how these wise guys from the East
arrived at this scene: They were willing to stop and ask directions.
They trusted their own vision —
having seen the star rising, studying the charts, knowing the tradition —
but they still stopped to ask, "Where is the newborn king of the Jews?"
Here are the wealthy and wise who were willing to stop and ask for help.

This is important because where Luke has shepherds,
symbols of the poor, the outcasts, and the alienated, as Jesus' first visitors,
Matthew has kings or wise ones, or astrologers.
Whatever their occupation was, they could afford a long trip
and brought gifts to boot.

Once again we see how all —
the down-and-out and the up-and-coming — are welcome.
Though wealthy and presumably wise,
they were also humble enough to stop and ask for directions.

TRUSTING OUR THOUGHTS, DARING OUR DREAMS

Another point worth remembering
is how, after visiting Jesus and presenting their gifts,
they had a dream that told them "not to return to Herod."
Returning to the king
would have been the politically correct and diplomatic thing to do.
But, instead, they returned to their country "by another way."

In addition to trusting their intelligence, they also trusted their instincts.
They trusted their knowledge about the star,
but they also trusted their dreams about the way they should return home.

Dreams may take us in a different direction than we had originally planned.
Dreams may make us find our way home by using alternative routes.

As we move beyond the manger to the mission it mandates,
we need to remember how important it is
to trust what we know but also what we feel —
to trust our knowledge, our thoughts, our prayers,
but also our dreams.

On second thought, it does matter. It does count.
As we continue beyond the manger,
we commit ourselves to making all our thoughts and all our words count
by bringing them to life in the language of love.

At this station God says to us,
"Don't worry about the gifts you bring; it is the thought that counts.
Trust me."

Tenth Station Prayer

We adore you, O Christ, and we bless you,
because by your holy birth you give hope to the world.

Thank you, O God,
for having second thoughts.
Your second thoughts about the world
did not cause doubt
but rather dreams to come true.

You did not keep these second thoughts to yourself.
Instead you put your thoughts into words,
especially a single Word,
a Word made flesh.
This Word, Jesus,
holds all the compassion and love,
the mercy and hope,
the joy and peace
you have in your sacred heart.

Stretch my heart and mind and soul, O God,
so that all people
might find a bent ear and a helping hand in me —
so that even those like Herod who are enemies of hope
might see a manifestation of your Word.

Make of me an incarnation of your second thoughts.
Make my life an answered prayer for someone in need.
Make me an instrument of your incarnation
where all thoughts count
and all prayers are answered.

+ *Amen.*

Eleventh Station

Presentation

Pillars of the Parish

When the time came for their purification according to the law of Moses,
they brought him up to Jerusalem to present him to the Lord.
Luke 2: 22

When I sit at this Station of the Presentation
I think of a woman I met many years ago.
"You know, Father," Louise whispered between coughs,
"I have to hold on a few more weeks
so I can see that great grandchild of mine.
God ain't gonna take me
until I hold that little girl in my arms."
Louise was sure the baby would be a girl.

Louise had lived in the same house for more than 80 years.
She was two years old when her parents moved the family
to this cozy wood-frame house now guarded by large evergreen trees.
Louise still remembered the day her father planted those trees.

The sound of the cancer that would eventually strangle her
rattled in her congested chest as she spoke softly but firmly.
Her spirit was not stifled by cancer's death grip.
"There's no reason to be down in the dumps
just because you feel a little punk," she told me that day.
"Besides, as long as I got something to look forward to,
there's nothing gonna keep me down."

She had pictures of all her children, grandchildren
and great grandchildren on the dresser by the bed.
One by one, I took them down and she told me each one's name.
"That's my granddaughter Marcia," Louise said.
"She's the one who is expecting in a few weeks."
Her eyes sparkled with expectation.
Where others might be anticipating only death,
Louise was passionately awaiting life.
I could tell that death had taken on a challenge
when deciding to come for Louise.
Her body would grow weary from the struggle,
but her spirit would never tire.

When I looked at the deep wrinkles on her face,
I could imagine how Simeon might have looked.
The faces of such holy ones are worn
by years of waiting for hope to be born.

Simeon is the patron saint
of all who are able to trust that God is very present
in all the dashed dreams and disappointments
they experience through the years.
In all the sorrows and all the tears
that leave scars upon their hearts,
and all the pain that tempts them to yield to despair,

they are seemingly impelled ever deeper into hope.
Simeon held on to hope because he spent his life
listening to the heartbeat of God in all the events of his life.

Then one day, after years of waiting,
Simeon was surprised by joy —
the joy of holding a child in his arms and seeing in his eyes
the face of God and the fulfillment of God's promises.

At this Presentation Station,
Mary and Joseph presented Jesus in the temple,
and an old man's dreams were realized.
Each day, we re-present Jesus in all we do, in all we are.
We re-present him in places of prayer and worship,
in our work and our relationships,
in our routine and our waiting.

Simeon trusted in that which was still hidden in God's heart.
That is the same lesson that a wise old woman named Louise taught me.
She held on long enough to hold that great grandchild in her arms.
A week or so after the baby was born,
her granddaughter Marcia brought her to Louise.
She held life in her arms one last time.
And though she didn't say, her eyes shouted it:
"Now, Master, you can dismiss your servant in peace;
you have fulfilled your word."

Louise died two weeks later.
But death had not won,
because Louise had witnessed God's saving deed
and displayed for me and for all to see
the light of love,
the tenacity of hope
and the courage to believe.

Anna: Beautiful Dreamer

Like Louise and Simeon,
Anna, the other person mentioned by name
at this Presentation Station,
shows us how tenacious yet tender hope can be.

You have heard the phrase, "Age before beauty."
It is usually uttered by a younger person opening a door for an elder.
But in Anna, age and beauty come together in a person
who reflected the truth of what someone once said:
"The grandeur of a great life lies in a fine finish."
Anna, the ancient widow,
was a beautiful dreamer headed for a fine finish.

"Age," Francis Bacon wrote, "appears best in four things —
old wood best to burn,
old wine to drink,
old friends to trust,
and old authors to read."
To this bit of wisdom, we might add a fifth:
"Age appears best in beautiful dreamers
who hold fast to their dreams."

Beauty ran in Anna's blood.
She is identified as the "daughter of Phanuel, of the tribe of Asher."
Phanuel, a name that rhymes with Emmanuel, means "face of God."
And Asher means "happy."
Anna, this 84-year-old widow who "never left the temple,"
is someone who reflects the "happy face of God."

Her genealogy may have contributed to her beauty,
but Anna is a "beautiful dreamer" because of her spirituality.
She is described as a prophet.

Again, prophecy ran in her family.
But her ability to prophesy was no doubt earned
through years of patient waiting and listening.
Married only seven years when her husband died,
she spent the rest of her life waiting and listening,
"worshipping day and night in fasting and prayer."

She overheard what her old friend Simeon was saying
about this child presented that day in the temple
and because the eyes of her heart were open,
she saw in Jesus the savior for whom she had been waiting.
Her excitement could not be contained
and she told everyone the good news.

Anna was not only beautiful, she was also wise.
Beauty, they say, is only skin deep.
Wisdom, though, is as deep as the soul.
Anna was wise not because she had lived a long life
but because she had listened a long time.
Wisdom does not necessarily come with age,
though the longer we live
the greater opportunity we have to make mistakes
and learn from them.
Wisdom comes from being in tune with God's Spirit,
being attentive to God's promise,
being present to God's presence.

What Shakespeare wrote of Cleopatra we might also say of Anna,
"Age cannot wither her."
Indeed, she was not withered or weathered but wise.
Because she had listened well to the voice of God
whispering within her own heart during all those years
she spent in the temple worshiping and praying,

Anna was awakened to the fulfillment of God's promise.
Wide awake with wisdom, Anna
"began to praise God and to speak about the child
to all who were looking for the redemption of Jerusalem."

The beautiful dreamer's dream had come true:
the reign of God was at hand.
The reign of God was held in the hands of Mary and Joseph.
Seeing this child, Anna knew she was headed for a fine finish.

From Holding On to Holding Us Up

Simeon and Anna were people modern-day pastors
might describe as "pillars of the parish."
With their prayerful, faithful witness,
they held up the temple community.

For a few days after Christmas some years ago,
I took a trip down memory lane.
On the map, memory lane was in Iowa.
I spent some time with two families in Centerville, Iowa,
the site of my first assignment as a priest.
The people of this parish — and particularly these two families —
were important in forming me as a priest.

In visiting with them that week after Christmas,
many names surfaced from those two brief years
I spent at the parish in the early 1980s.
Among these names were two women named Anna.
Both Anna D and Anna G had been widows for years
by the time I met them.
But every morning, Anna D would pick up Anna G,
and they would unlock the church for morning Mass
and pray the rosary.

Anna D was the more dominant personality of the two.
She was a tall woman who was never shy
in offering her opinion about parish matters or sermons.
Anna G was the quiet one, a small woman,
her back slightly bent from the weight of so many years,
and she always followed a step or two behind Anna D.

Like the Anna in the presentation story,
Anna D and Anna G dedicated their lives to the parish.
From serving as sacristans to singing in the funeral choir,
from leading the rosary before the morning Mass
to leading people back to church after they had been away for a while,
these two widows gave witness with their lives of the presence of God.

Who are the pillars of our own life's journey —
the people who have supported us and encouraged us
and challenged us in our own life of faith?
As we identify these pillars we've met along the way,
I suspect they all have this much in common:
They allowed the presence of Christ
to "grow in size and strength" within them;
they were "filled with wisdom
and the grace of God was upon them."

Though some of these pillars will have long since passed away,
they do not live among the ruins
but rather serve as part of the foundation
that holds up the temples of our hearts.
Give thanks for them today as you go to this temple to pray.
And there, like Simeon and Anna, may you say
without fear or trembling or conceit,
"Now you can dismiss your servant in peace,
you have fulfilled your word."

Eleventh Station Prayer

We adore you, O Christ, and we bless you,
because by your holy birth you give hope to the world.

Grandmother God,
tender and compassionate,
understanding and forgiving,
cradle me in your arms this day,
balance me on your knee,
hold me in your lap
and never let me go.

Like your servants
Simeon and Anna,
even as I grow old,
may I never grow tired
of spending time with you in prayer.

Though I may become timid at times in my witness,
may I never limit the possibilities of the wonders
awaiting me around the corner.

I present my life with all its worries and wonders,
with all its scars and sacred and scary moments,
with all its hope and all its hurts
to you,
my Grandma God.
You hold my life in your gentle hands.

Into your hands, I commend my spirit.

+ Amen.

Twelfth Station

Evasion

THE GREAT ESCAPE

When they had departed, behold an angel of the Lord
appeared to Joseph in a dream and said,
"Rise, take the child and his mother, and flee to Egypt,
and remain there until I tell you...."
Matthew 2: 13

My sister told me that a few years ago
when she and her husband wanted to sell their home,
they planted a statue of St. Joseph
upside down in their front yard.
My sister swears by this practice.
They sold their house very quickly.

Evidently this practice is widespread.
When I was in a Catholic religious goods store recently,
they had a stack of "St. Joseph Kits for Selling Your Home"
on their front counter — the place where merchandisers

put the impulse-buying products.
I glanced at the contents while I was waiting in line.
The box contained a statue and a prayer to be said
while planting St. Joseph upside down in the ground.

I'm not sure why it is important to plant Joseph upside down,
but as a priest in my community put it,
"We've got the poor guy standing on his head."
Still, I like this image of Joseph
standing on his head.
No doubt there were many times
when Joseph felt like God was making him
stand on his head.

This Twelfth Station is one of those times.
In another dream —
Joseph would never be mistaken for a sound sleeper —
an angel appears and tells Joseph
to wake up the family and flee.
This is the great escape,
the graced evasion,
as Joseph the protector saves his family
from Herod's terrorism.

The Power of Dreams

The Holy Family had to travel far from home
to escape the horror of Herod's vengeance.
This story of their flight into Egypt
is instructive in our search for hope.
Remember how Moses, prophet of the first covenant,
was called to lead his people
out of slavery in Egypt to the promised land.

Jesus, Messiah of the new covenant,
is called out of Egypt after Herod's death
to lead all people out of the slavery of sin
to the promised land of everlasting life.
The stories of both Moses and Jesus begin
with a person of faith named Joseph
who trusted in the power of his dreams.

For our ancestors in faith, it was Jacob's son, Joseph,
known for his multicolored coat and his many dreams,
who was sold into slavery in Egypt by his envious brothers.
He went, or was sent by God, into Egypt because of his dreams.

Joseph, the carpenter, likewise followed his dreams
by taking his family into flight
in the middle of the night
to find refuge in Egypt.
Because Joseph trusted in his dreams,
the life of the infant Jesus was spared
and the story of our salvation had the chance to unfold.

The Gospels actually record three dreams of Joseph,
who would settle his family in Nazareth
after this frightening ordeal of flight.
In the first dream, the angel says to Joseph,
"Get up, take the child and his mother, and flee to Egypt."
In the second dream that occurs after Herod's death,
the angel returns in another dream and says to Joseph,
"Get up, take the child and his mother and go to the land of Israel."
But on the way back home,
Joseph has yet another dream that warns him
not to return to his old hometown
but to "make his home in a town called Nazareth."

In responding to these dreams,
Joseph offers us a practical process for following our own dreams.
The first thing we must do is "Get up!"
In fact, those are the first words the angel says to Joseph.
We need to "Get up!"
We can't stay under the covers,
content to catch a few extra minutes of sleep.
When God's dream for us becomes clear,
it's like an alarm clock that shakes us from our sleep.
We must get out of bed,
wake up our sleepy head and heart, and follow.

Once we are awake,
we must take our family, our community,
those we love the most, with us.
Dreams are not simply for our own personal fulfillment,
our own personal gain,
our own fame or fortune.
True dreams include those we love,
those who form and fashion a sacred connection.
True dreams are inclusive.
True prophets and dreamers are those who take the rest of us
to a new land of promise and peace.

The third step in this process of following God's dream for us
is to go where God tells us to go.
Because of Herod's vengeance,
Joseph is told to go to a place where he probably wouldn't dare go
if he were relying on his own resources.
After all, Egypt was the place from which his ancestors
had escaped slavery.
But now he is told to go back to Egypt
because it will be a place of refuge and safety.

Joseph will stay with his family in Egypt
until God tells him the coast is clear.
This is the fourth step in the journey of following our dreams.
We are to stay in the place where we find refuge
until God tells us it's time to go.
Here we must trust, as Joseph did, that God's time is not our time.
We must trust that God knows what time it is
and when the coast is clear.

The final step in following our dreams
is to believe that God will show us the way home.
Joseph was going to take Mary and Jesus back to his old hometown,
but God had other plans.
Now Joseph will make his home in Nazareth.
This is the place where Joseph, Mary and Jesus
will settle down and make their home.

A Place Called Home

Tradition holds that Joseph was a carpenter by trade,
barely scratching out a living,
desiring nothing more than living a simple life.
But because the woman he loved was chosen by God
to be the vessel of blessing through which the incarnation
of God's love would take flesh,
Joseph was thrust into salvation's spotlight.

This station challenges us to take stock of the gifts we have
to create a safe and sacred place we call home.
From material possessions to spiritual resources,
an inventory of our belongings invites us
to take a serious look at how we are using our gifts
to offer one another safe shelter from the storms of life.

As we witnessed on September 11, 2001,
in times of great terror and inexplicable evil,
the power of love is found in our willingness
to risk our lives to help those in need.
This is what Joseph symbolizes at this station:
Grounded in prayer, and at great risk to himself,
he engineered the great escape to save his family from terrorism.

We may not have money to burn,
but like Joseph, who listened to his dream
and took Mary and Jesus out of harm's way by escaping to Egypt,
we do have faith to burn.

As Joseph has shown in previous stations,
he puts his future in the hands of God,
packs up his family and flees to Egypt.
Joseph can do this because he believes
that the name Emmanuel evokes not only a promise
but a presence — a real presence.
There is no suffering or pain,
no rejection or revilement,
no abandonment or abuse that is alien to God.
In every age of human history where evil runs rampant,
the name Emmanuel shatters the illusion that God is absent.

Isn't this what we discovered in ourselves and others
on September 11, 2001?
Pundits and priests and politicians boldly proclaimed
that we would be changed forever by the events of that fateful day.
Whether this is true is open to debate.
But didn't we find, at least for a time,
a more generous and compassionate spirit
toward others who were in need

after the horrific events of that day?
And if God is love — unconditional love —
then don't we find in the love and valor and compassion
we saw expressed that day,
and the days following the terrorist attacks,
the presence of God?

In every family where misunderstanding
seeks to separate parents from children,
mothers from fathers, sisters from brothers,
the name Emmanuel seeks to draw the family back together
in fidelity and forgiveness.
In every personal life where despair has pushed one to the brink,
the name Emmanuel reaches out to give us hope.

While we normally perceive Joseph
as a simple craftsman, a carpenter,
I can see why the practice of planting
a statue of Joseph upside down in one's front lawn
when one is trying to sell one's home
is more than a practice of piety.
It makes some good common spiritual sense.
Since St. Joseph guarded the real presence,
it should come as no surprise
that he's handy in real estate as well.
Joseph was a real estate agent —
an agent for grace,
for change,
for a place to call home.

Twelfth Station Prayer

We adore you, O Christ, and we bless you,
because by your holy birth you give hope to the world.

Loving God, the evil in the world
sometimes causes my head to spin and my heart to race.
Terrorism turns the world upside down,
and I wonder what has become of your grace
and if we will ever be the same again.

Your servant Joseph knew terror.
He knew fear, but he did not allow his fright
to keep him from seeing the light of your promise.
Paying attention to your call,
he took flight with his family
to save Jesus from the wrath of Herod.

When events beyond my control turn my world upside down
and I feel trapped underground,
give me the courage to see your presence as the essence of my hope.

Ground my being in the truth of your love.
May I never grow weary in extending
my compassion to those in need.
St. Joseph, intercede for me and protect the members of my family —
and the entire human family — from all that is evil.

St. Joseph, patron of the dying,
be with those who are at the moment of death.
Hold those who are the victims of violence and terrorism.
Embrace those who are not ready to die.
Send me the grace of God to meet the terrors of our day
with the power of God's love.

+Amen.

The Restoration

THE LONG JOURNEY HOME

When Herod died, behold an angel of the Lord
appeared in a dream to Joseph in Egypt, saying,
"Rise, take the child and his mother,
and go to the land of Israel...."
Matthew 2: 19

Joseph's vocation is to make sure that Mary and Jesus
always have a roof over their heads.
At this Thirteenth Station we remember how an angel once again
appears to Joseph in a dream and tells him it's time to go home:
"Those who sought the child's life are dead."
Matthew doesn't say how long they were in exile in Egypt.
We can only assume that while they were away,
Joseph provided shelter for his family.
And when God told him it was time to go,
"he rose and took the child and his mother, and went to the land of Israel."

Reflecting on Joseph's vocation as
protector and provider for the Holy Family,
I am reminded of my own father whose name is the same: Joseph.

One piece of wisdom from my dad that I have never forgotten is this:
When the oil light comes on in the car,
pull off to the side of the road, turn off the engine,
and put oil in the (adjective deleted) car!

I received this bit of advice some years ago
after I drove for a while with the oil light
on the dashboard demanding my attention.
"Don't you know," my father said at the time,
"you can burn up the (adjective deleted) engine
if you don't check the oil and make sure it's not low."
So now, I check the oil religiously
and have it changed ritually every three thousand miles.

I suspect that Jesus learned lessons such as these
from his foster father, Joseph.
Regarding the ancient practice
of checking and changing the oil, for example,
could it be that Jesus learned this truth from Joseph, who —
from what we gather in the three Gospel stories
where an angel appears to the guardian of Jesus in a dream
and tells him what to do —
often burned the midnight oil.
Wise are those who check and change the oil regularly
to make sure their lamps are burning brightly.

Checking the Oil

As we near the end of our journey,
if we haven't done it before this —

and I can hear my father saying,
"You've come this far and haven't checked the oil?" —
now would be a good time to do it.
If the oil in the lamp of commitment is burning low,
perhaps it's time to change the oil.

We might check our supply of three kinds of oil:
the oil of prayer, the oil of compassion and the oil of gladness.

First, there's the oil of prayer that lubricates our souls
and keeps us running smoothly.
No matter how busy we get or how many starts and stops we make,
the oil of prayer fuels the engine of our desire to serve.
The time we spend filling our soul
with the oil of prayer in silence and contemplation
will give us the energy, the stamina, the spirit
and the love to live truly and to serve others.

In this work of service,
we dispense the oil of compassion.
If the oil of prayer is like the motor oil
we put in our car to keep the engine running smoothly,
we might compare the oil of compassion with the "Oil of Olay" —
the kind of oil that makes our skin so soft.
Being compassionate means we're sensitive to the pain of others.
When we have thick skin, we can take a lot before we feel the pain.
The oil of compassion makes our skin sensitive.
Tough skin is for those
who don't want to feel their pain or the suffering of others.
By contrast, the oil of compassion softens our skins
and is an ointment for our wounds.
And when we minister from our own wounds,
we are more prepared to embrace the wounds of others.

We might also check the storeroom
to see how much oil of gladness we have on hand.
When our tank is full of the oil of gladness,
we anticipate meeting God with a smile on our face.
The oil of gladness is captured in that Christmas song,
"You'd better watch out; you better not pout!"
People who embrace hope are always on the lookout,
watching out for the coming of God into our lives.
People who have hope do not pout or brood, grimace or frown,
but rather are about receiving with joy the mercy God has in store for us.

HURRICANE LAMPS

The challenge of this Thirteenth Station
is to make sure there is enough oil in our lamps
so that we might be for our families and friends
what Joseph was for his family:
a hurricane lamp in the world's window.

Hurricanes of violence and war rage against us;
hurricanes of oppression and injustice seek to overwhelm us;
but in the eye of the hurricane there is calm and a quiet assurance.
The eye of the hurricane
casts a glance of gracious trust in a God who saves.
The eye of the hurricane offers a world teetering on the brink
of annihilation a different point of view, a unique perspective:
a hope at the end of the world.
These holy oils keep that fire of love burning.

There is an expression we sometimes use
to draw comparisons between people and events.
We might say, for example, "Last year's Super Bowl
couldn't hold a candle to this year's game!"

Or this book or that speaker or this movie
can't hold a candle to that one.
We mean that the one who can't hold a candle
to the other is inferior, second-rate, mediocre.

At times we even apply this comparison to matters of faith.
For example, I think of someone like my patron, Joseph,
and I wonder if my faith can hold a candle to his faith?
Joseph appears as one of those whose faith is strong,
whose love is unlimited, whose hope endures.

When the light of the world broke through the barrier
between heaven and earth to bathe the planet
in the redeeming stream of God's grace and mercy,
Joseph was chosen to hold and protect the light.
But Joseph is only a model of what all of us are called to be:
candle holders.
We all hold the candle of faith in our hearts.
We all are redeemed.

With this flame of faith illuminating our past,
we are not afraid to look at mistakes or failures,
losses or lamentations,
because we know we are redeemed.
When life has knocked us to the floor,
we rise to our feet, brush ourselves off,
and keep going on — through the force of our faith.

With this flame of faith lighting the way,
we can walk into the future as Joseph did with courage and with hope.
As long as we guard that flame of faith,
so long as we hold the candle high against the coming of the night,
we shall find our way home.

BEACONS OF HOPE

When I think of people in my life who were such beacons of hope,
I think of my dad's mother, Grandma Anna.

I remember the first time my grandma took me to see Santa Claus.
I don't remember how old I was, but I recall
the hope and excitement I was feeling.
I was young enough (or am old enough now!)
to remember that the streetcars were still operating in St. Louis.
Since my grandma didn't drive, we took a streetcar to another suburb
where Santa was perched on a huge platform in an open-air square.

We waited in line for what seemed like hours to me.
But as we approached the platform where Santa was sitting,
I began to get nervous.
He looked larger than I imagined.
His long white beard and red coat seemed mysterious and even menacing.
The closer we got, the more afraid I became.
(It was the same sort of experience I had
when I went to confession for the first time!)
When I was only two or three children away
from sitting on the great man's lap,
I started to cry and to scream.
Grandma tried to calm me down, but she couldn't.
I just screamed all the louder.
Grandma and a kindly elf
escorted me down the steps and back into the crowd.

Then Grandma did what Grandmas are supposed to do:
She took me over to Woolworth's, which had a soda fountain.
She bought me some hot chocolate
and asked me the same question old Santa was going to ask:
"What do you want for Christmas?"

This is an image of God,
an image of hope, that this station suggests
in the person of Joseph, protector of Jesus.
It is the image of a God who,
like Santa or Grandma, says to us:
"What do you want?"

When we are in the presence of such beacons of hope,
we sense how the sparks fly when stories of old are told.
We sense how these sparks from the stories of salvation history
resemble the stars that shone in the night sky
when the angels announced the birth of Christ.
We feel God's favor that will fill us
with the light of new promises and new possibilities
because this birth of hope
challenges us to believe in the light of our own goodness,
to see the light of God's truth growing within us,
the light of God's promises that will be fulfilled through us
if only we cling to the light
and let go of our fear of the night.

As we journey in hope,
the fog of our fear will be lifted,
and we will follow our dreams
to a place called home.

And we say at this station,
"Give us hope" —
the hope that will sustain us
and give us strength to make it the rest of the way
home.

Thirteenth Station Prayer

We adore you, O Christ, and we bless you,
because by your holy birth you give hope to the world.

God of Light,
when darkness hovers all around us
and the darkness within threatens to overwhelm me,
remind me to check and change the oil
in the lamp of my soul.

When another is far from home,
let me be a light in the window to welcome her home.
When another feels forsaken,
let me be the oil of prayer to console him.
When another is broken,
let me be the oil of compassion to help her heal.
When another is sad,
let me be the oil of gladness to help him know joy again.

In this time of prayer,
may I guard this flame with care
so that I may be a beacon of hope
to someone who yearns to come home.

+Amen.

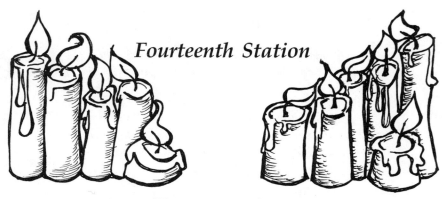

Fourteenth Station

Reputation

INCREASING FAITH

He went and dwelt in a city called Nazareth,
that what was spoken by the prophets might be fulfilled,
"He shall be called a Nazarene."
Matthew 2: 23

A few years ago my brother Bob bought my parents
a book for Christmas called *The World Book of Nassals*.
Supposedly every person in the world who has the same
last name as my family was included in this book.
There was, of course, at least one glaring omission.
I wasn't included in the book!
My name and address did not appear.
Since we suspect the company that produced the book
gleaned telephone directories from around the world
to gather the list of names,
I could only surmise that I moved around so much
they couldn't track me down.

Matthew's Gospel begins by tracking down the ancestors of Jesus
— at least on Joseph's side — and his description of the details
surrounding Jesus' birth conclude with this Fourteenth Station
where Joseph sets up shop in a town called Nazareth.

When one reads the Gospel passage of Jesus' genealogy,
it is like reading a phone book — not very interesting.
The only thing that might spark a hint of interest
when the passage of Jesus' family tree is proclaimed in a liturgical setting
is how often the one who reads it aloud
trips over the pronunciation of some of these names.
Theologically, of course, this genealogy is important
because it reflects Jesus' roots,
those famous and sometimes infamous folks of whom he is a descendant.
Since it was written in a patristic time, from a paternalistic point of view,
most of those who are listed are men.
However, there are four women listed (besides Mary) in the genealogy:
Tamar, Rahab, Ruth and the wife of Uriah.

Some scholars have suggested that these four women
are listed because they were sinners
and so reflected the need for redemption brought by Jesus.
But, of course, any number of the men listed
could also fall into this category of sinners.
King David, for one, in addition to slinging his slingshot,
also had a few flings of infidelity.

But scholars also suggest that the four women are named
because in very specific ways they furthered God's plan of salvation.
In the book of Genesis, the widow Tamar disguised herself as a prostitute
and ended up getting pregnant by Judah.
In salvation's scheme of things,
Tamar was one of those chosen to fulfill God's promise to Abraham
about descendants "as numerous as the stars."

In the book of Joshua,
Rahab is reflected as a woman of great courage
who risked her own safety to provide sanctuary for two of Joshua's spies.
Ruth, also a widow,
united with Boaz so that the Davidic line could continue.
And the wife of Uriah is one of those with whom
King David had a fling after he sent her husband into battle,
ordering him to be on the front line so that he was sure to be killed.
After Uriah fell in a heap, David married his wife,
and she became the mother of Solomon.
Sounds a lot like a soap opera.
Or a family tree.

I suspect if we were to trace our family of origin,
we would find a few folks whose reputations
we would not like to hold up to a spotlight of scrutiny.
But this is Matthew's point in beginning his Gospel
with Jesus' genealogy: that the family of Jesus is a very human family
comprised of saints and sinners, heroes and villains,
prophetic figures and one-dimensional stick figures
whom some members of the family would rather break in two
than mention their names.

Tracing the roots of Jesus' family tree
reminds us yet again that Jesus was born into a family
that had more than a few rotten apples on its tree —
but they were not rotten to the core.
Rather, God worked through all the members of Jesus' family tree
to get the earth ready for the most remarkable revelation of all:
Emmanuel, God is with us.

This Fourteenth Station offers an opportunity to trace our own roots,
to remember not only the ones we reverence
as good and holy and upstanding,

but also those who down through the years
have been considered "bad apples" on the family tree.
We reverence the family ties that bind us to one another and to God,
who works through all to further the plan of salvation.

A Theology of Relativity

It is said that when someone asked Albert Einstein's wife
if she understood the theory of relativity, she said,
"No, but I know my husband, and you can trust him."

Albert Einstein gave us a "theory of relativity"
but God gives us a "theology of relativity."
We are all related.
And the more we know about another, the easier it is to trust that person.

The theology of relativity
develops from our respect and reverence for our blood relatives.
This is where our recognition of relativity begins.
Paul dresses up this theology of relativity
in an image most of us can identify with: new clothes for Christmas.
"Clothe yourself," Paul writes to the Colossians,
"with heartfelt mercy, with kindness, humility, meekness and patience."
These are the threads
woven into the garment of grace we receive at baptism.
These garments of grace are "hand-me-down clothes" —
something that those of us familiar with family life know something about.
But these "hand-me-down clothes" are handed down from on high,
made with "silver threads and golden needles" by the hand of God.

Paul isn't focused just on the blood family here.
Because of the love we have found in our family life,
we are to spread it around.
Because we have the blood of Christ flowing through our veins,

we are to recognize the presence of Christ in every person.
God's theology of relativity means we see Christ in one another
and see the image of God in every human being.

Do you remember the story about Mary and Joseph
noticing that Jesus was missing as they returned home
from visiting and vacationing in Jerusalem?
They found their son in the temple.
Most of us have little difficulty finding Jesus in the temple,
or the sanctuary, or the church, or the wafer or the wine.
Our difficulty is seeing and recognizing Jesus
on the street or at the supermarket, at the mall or at the office.

Recall how before Mary and Joseph found Jesus in the temple,
they looked for him among their relatives and friends.
This Fourteenth Station invites us to look again and to see Jesus
among those whose company we keep on a regular basis.
But this station is also inviting us to extend
and live this theology of relativity
until the entire human family becomes a holy family.

This theology of relativity encourages us to see
we are all blood brothers and sisters who clothe ourselves
with the "hand-me-down clothes"
of mercy and meekness, kindness and compassion,
patience and perseverance, forgiveness and faith.
When we "don" this "grace apparel,"
we live in such a way that people will know
and see that Christ dwells within us and among us.

THE INCREDIBLE SHRINKING MAN

In this theology of relativity,
one of the blood relatives we have mentioned often is Joseph.

His name means "increasing faith."
Joseph's name offers us a prayer: Increase our faith, O God.

The quiet life of this carpenter from Nazareth
is surrounded by mystery.
He was a just man who had a reputation for holiness.
But after the story about Jesus' disappearance in the temple,
Joseph disappears from Scripture.
He vanishes into thin air.
There is not another mention of this man.
Where did he go? How and when did he die?
We don't know.
Was he still alive when Jesus left home to begin his public ministry?
What lessons about life did Jesus learn from Joseph?

Joseph is the Scripture's "incredible shrinking man."
He shrinks from the scene so that the only incidents
we have recorded about Joseph surround the time of Jesus' birth.
But it is in his shrinking, in his *decreasing*,
in his disappearing, that we may discover
the reason why we honor the memory of Joseph.
As his name implies,
it is because he spent his life *increasing* his faith
that we don't recall his accomplishments, honors, deeds or words.
All we remember is his faith.
His fame decreased as his faith increased.

Joseph spent his life getting out of the way
so that God's way, God's will, could prevail.
As we have seen throughout these Stations of the Crib,
in the Scripture passages where Joseph is mentioned,
he is depicted as a compassionate and caring carpenter
who is devoted to Mary and Jesus.
Even when he assumed that Mary had betrayed him,

he didn't want to punish her by exposing her to the religious authorities.
In the tradition of his father in faith, Abraham,
"hoping against hope" that God's promises to him would be fulfilled,
Joseph's ever-increasing faith allowed him
to accept his dream and believe the angel's promise
that it was by the Holy Spirit that Mary conceived this child.

Joseph didn't ask for a second opinion.
He didn't have to research any precedents
for such an astonishing case of divine intervention
because he knew the story of Abraham and Sarah by heart.
So, on those three occasions we've already noted
when an angel appeared to him and told him what to do,
when he awoke from these dreams,
he simply did as the angel of God directed him.

The Church also honors Joseph as patron saint of the dying.
Joseph is just the kind of companion we need on our pilgrimage
as we seek to decrease our fears and allow our faith to increase.

Perhaps most of all we might take notice
of how Joseph's identity is defined in terms of relationship:
He is in relationship to Mary as her husband;
he is in relationship to Jesus as protector of the body of Christ
when Jesus was young.
We remember Joseph not so much for who he was
but for who he was in relationship to those he loved,
to those he cared for,
to the God he trusted and the people entrusted to him.
Joseph reminds us we cannot make this journey alone.
We need to be in relationship.
We need God and we need to be in relationship with others
if we are going to complete this journey of hope.

Fourteenth Station Prayer

We adore you, O Christ, and we bless you,
because by your holy birth you give hope to the world.

Increase my faith, O God.
Help me to tame my shrewd ego
that desires only fame.
You claim me as your own,
and that is all the acclaim I need.

You have made me a member of your family tree
because you have made me in your image.
Though I am aware at times how great my sin is,
how far I have fallen from the tree of life,
you remind me I am not rotten to the core.

Far from it.
In fact and in faith,
because I am made in your image,
I can cling to this tree of life with hope
and never fear falling from grace.

Scatter seeds of hope
on the landscape of our world
so that all family trees may grow
to transform the world
into a forest of peace.
In such a forest as this,
all can find shelter and shade
in your outstretched arms.

+Amen.

Fifteenth Station

Dedication

THE WORK OF OUR HEARTS AND HANDS

The child grew and became strong, filled with wisdom;
and the favor of God was upon him.
Luke 2: 40

'Twas the day after Christmas
and all through house,
wrapping paper was scattered
but it hardly mattered.
Ribbons and bows were flung far and wide
as the family sat together by the crackling fireside.

I suppose there are some families that wait to pick up
the wrapping paper until the day after Christmas or even later.
But not my family.
My dad, with a trash bag in hand, goes through the living room
immediately after all the gifts are opened and picks up
all the discarded wrapping paper, as Mom inevitably says,
"Save the bows!"

Some people not only save the bows but also the wrapping paper —
not so much to recycle it for the next Christmas,
but because they value the time and care it took
to wrap a package as part of the gift.

This journey of hope we are on
is about redeeming the smallest of things.
When we are grateful
for the small things in life that we sometimes overlook,
we learn life's largest lessons and receive our greatest gifts.

For example, have you ever found a dime on the sidewalk
and thought yourself the richest person in the world?
For most of us, finding a dime will not make our day.
The old line, "Buddy, can you spare a dime?"
is no longer a fiscally responsible form of begging
since a dime won't buy much anymore.
Yet some long-distance phone companies
do advertise that for ten cents a minute you can call home.
So, for a dime, you can phone home
and tell all the news, provided you talk very quickly.

When we say some things are "a dime a dozen,"
we mean they're not worth very much,
that they are so common, so ordinary, that their value is depleted.
But this Fifteenth Station reminds us how valuable our ordinary time
with family and friends truly is.
With a dime, we might buy some time with our family
or make a connection with an old friend.

Our Scriptures don't tell us much about the years
between Jesus' birth and the beginning of his public ministry —
except for the time he played hooky from his family
and was found days later in the temple teaching

the Scribes and Pharisees a thing or two —
a foreshadowing of things to come.
All we know is that he "grew in size and strength,
filled with wisdom, and the grace of God was upon him."
So we might assume that in those very ordinary years
the Holy Family embraced the grace of God's presence among them,
which made their lives extraordinary.

The greatest of gifts is found in the love we share.
We can't buy this love, but we can make an investment,
and it doesn't even cost us a dime.
All it costs us is a little time to share memories and dreams,
to reverence the small things of our lives and our relationships.

So maybe at this station, the line
"Buddy, can you spare a dime?" becomes
"Family, friends, can you spare some time?"
This is what we might call the work of our hearts:
spending time in the company of those we love and
finding that the peace reigning in our hearts
is really not so rare after all.
In the process we make it less rare in our world.
We make it very ordinary.
We make this peace so ordinary that it becomes "a dime a dozen."

THE WORK OF OUR HANDS

If spending time with those we love is the work of our hearts,
then at this last station we also pay attention to the work of our hands
that gives our lives more than a measure of meaning and purpose.

A few years ago I was driving to St. Louis after a retreat in Wisconsin
to celebrate my mom and dad's fiftieth wedding anniversary.
I was just about to cross the Illinois border when I heard a loud noise,

and the car began to rumble and roll as if it had a life of its own.
A blowout at 70 miles an hour while passing a semi
is certainly a wake-up call.
I steered the car to the side of the road, and when I examined
the front right tire, there wasn't much tire left to examine.
It was shredded.

Among my least favorite activities is changing a tire
on the shoulder of a busy interstate.
Fortunately, the spare had air in it,
though when they call the spare a "doughnut" tire,
they certainly describe it accurately.
The spare tire seemed only slightly larger than the glazed doughnut
I had for breakfast that morning.
But again good fortune was with me
as I found a car dealer at the very next exit.

It was after 5:00 when the blowout occurred,
and even though the garage was closed, the parts department was still open.
A young woman whose name tag said "Tracy" was most helpful
in my securing a used tire to take me the rest of the way to St. Louis.
Tracy stopped what she was doing and focused all her attention on me.
I had the feeling that I was, at that moment,
the most important person in this young woman's life.

Though it might have been the end of a long day at the end of a long week,
Tracy never gave the impression that my predicament was a burden to her.
And her motivation for being so generous
in giving her time and her service had nothing to do
with my being a potential return customer.
She saw my Kansas license plate. She knew I was just passing through.
Tracy treated me with such kindness,
and a young man she called "Cisco" found the tire

and put it on my car with such routine efficiency and expertise
that hospitality to a stranded stranger on the interstate
was "all in a day's work."

In fact, Cisco was so efficient in getting me back on the road quickly
that I didn't have a chance to pick up from them
a story or two for the road.
But then, as you've guessed by now, Tracy and Cisco are the story.
I didn't have to ask them, "Do you like your work?"
because it was evident in the way they treated me.
They captured what Dorothy Day once wrote about the Catholic Worker:
"Hospitality means more than serving a meal, opening a door,
or offering a bed. It means opening our hearts to others."
In their very simple yet sacred way,
Tracy and Cisco opened their hearts to me.

The Work We Do

Can we say, "I love my work"
and say it with such conviction and commitment
that we see the work of our lives not as a means to another end,
not as something we do until something better comes along,
but rather as something that is very sacred to us?
I love what I do. I love who I am.
The doing is an expression of the being;
our work is a visible representation of our invisible passion,
a divine manifestation of our very human lives.

Though we don't know much about how he approached his work,
we might assume that Joseph was well-known in his hometown
for his skill and passion as a carpenter.
Remember that when Jesus returned home
after his first missionary experience,
he was identified by the hometown crowd according to his father's craft:

"Isn't this the carpenter's son?"

I suspect that if someone asked Joseph about his vocation as a carpenter,
Joseph would have replied, "I love my work,"
because he did his work with love.
I suspect that Joseph the worker left his signature
in the sawdust of his carpenter's shop
and on every piece of furniture he built —
just as certainly as farmers leave their signatures on the fields they plow,
as potters leave their signatures on the vases they create,
cooks on the meals they prepare,
writers on their books,
spiritual directors on the souls of those they accompany,
massage therapists on the bodies they touch,
teachers on the students they teach,
janitors on the floors they sweep,
landscapers on the lawns they mow,
foresters on the trees they plant,
accountants on the bills they pay.

All work is sacred when the work is accomplished with great love.
Then our work makes visible the presence and power of love —
as visible as it was to me when Tracy and Cisco
left their signature on my memory as they helped me get back on the road.
Meister Eckhart said,
"The outward work will never be puny if the inward work is great."
Then, when the work of our lives is complete,
we will find there is a welcome mat at the end of the world
that says, "Welcome Home."

Welcome Hope

But while there is still work to do,
we are encouraged to stand in the darkness of the world's discontent

and call the place where we stand *home*.
This is not a comfortable or easy place to stand.
How do we respond to the suffering in our lives and our world?
As these stations have suggested, the story of the incarnation
means that God advises us to make ourselves at home in the mess.
This is what Jesus did.
He puts down the welcome mat at those places
in our lives when we thought our world would end and says,
"Don't worry. Welcome home."

We are the work of God's hands, God's heart.
As time flies and the world spins 'round like a potter's wheel,
God is shaping, molding, creating us into a work of the heart.
God's hands are tough from being patient with us
but tender from still hoping in us.

Though we often have clay feet and even harder hearts,
or are like clay pots that fall from the shelf and shatter —
broken by our sin and our shame, by our jealousies and our fears,
by the turf we seek to protect and the tenderness we fail to show —
God never gives up on us.
When we are in the middle of a mess,
God is like the famous sculptor Rodin, who advised his students
when they looked at a piece that just didn't look right
to stop picking at it, "making little changes here and there."
Instead, he told them, "drop it on the floor and see what it looks like then."

Our challenge as hope seekers
is to stand on the welcome mat of the world
and welcome hope into our hearts.
These stations underscore the truth that there is no turmoil or tragedy,
calamity or crisis that God does not comprehend.
God knows what we suffer and God responds.

So wherever you are,
roll out the welcome mat and make yourself "at hope."
God has. God does. God always will.
That is the mystery and the message of the Incarnation:
God is with us at every station and every step of the way —
until that day when God says to us,
"Welcome home."

Fifteenth Station Prayer:

We adore you, O Christ, and we bless you,
because by your holy birth you give hope to the world.

Gracious God, I consecrate my life,
the work of my heart,
the work of my hands,
to you.

I am, O God, a fragile vessel with feet of clay.
I stay in the same place,
longing and praying for the day
when all shall be one.

But you remind me, O God,
that you made me to make a difference in the world.
So wherever this journey of life takes me,
may I always remember to bring
the welcome mat with me.

When my life seems out of sorts,
when terror rages around me and anger burns inside me,
when grief consumes my dreams
and guilt smothers my desire
and shame lays claim to my soul,
you put out the welcome mat and say,
"Welcome hope."

You, O God, made yourself at home
in the mess and mayhem of the world.
May I find my place here too
even as I pray for the day
when you welcome me home.

+Amen.

Epilogue

Away from the Manger to Mission
The Tree of Hope

On my sabbatical last year
I stopped at the Oklahoma City National Memorial
dedicated to the victims of the bombing of the Federal Building.
Prior to September 11, 2001,
this was the site of the worst act of terrorism committed on American soil.

The Gates of Time are the first things you see
when you walk through this memorial in Oklahoma City.
On one monument, the time 9:01 AM is engraved in marble;
on the opposite side where the Federal building once stood,
9:03 AM is etched in stone.
These Gates of Time mark the minute before
and the minute after the bomb went off.
In between, in a single minute, life changed.
Death came.

In between these gates is a reflection pool that once was the street
where the Ryder truck carrying the bomb was parked

and a lawn filled with 168 empty chairs,
symbolizing each of the men, women and children
killed in the explosion of hate at 9:02 AM on April 19, 1995.

One cannot imagine the horror of that moment.
The museum dramatically tells the story
through news footage and interviews with survivors.
Tears come easily as one views
the pictures of the dead in the Gallery of Honor
and the displays of keys, shoes and watches
that belonged to the deceased
and the scarred stuffed animals that belonged to the children
killed in the bombing.
They are sad, stunning reminders
of the simple possessions of everyday life
and how in one, brief, blinding minute, it all was taken away.

For one dark, chaotic minute, violence and terrorism won out.
But the monument and museum in Oklahoma City proclaim clearly
that violence and terrorism never have the last word.
Indeed, the last room you visit in the museum is called "Hope."
This room looks out over the site of the explosion,
the field of empty chairs, the gates of time
and the reflection pool.
The room, filled with images of hope and life, asks the visitor,
Do we dare to hope?

These Stations of the Crib have sought to remind us
how hope is born right here, right now,
because of the incarnation of Jesus Christ.
Our God seeks to stand with us at all the stations of our lives.
Most of us appreciate a "down-to-earth" kind of person —
one we can relate to "face-to-face,"

someone who can look us in the eye and help us see
when we don't see "eye to eye,"
one who stands nose-to-nose, toe-to-toe and shoulder-to-shoulder with us.
This is what God intends to do with us and for us every step of our lives.
And because of our "down-to-earth" God,
we are not afraid to hope.

This was certainly the message I took with me
from visiting the Oklahoma City memorial.
It is a message found in what they call "the Survivor's Tree,"
which stands on a hill overlooking the field of empty chairs.
This ancient elm tree was only a few hundred feet from Ground Zero.
It survived the blast from the bomb, the shattered glass and debris.
It has survived and is a symbol
for the people of Oklahoma City and the world
of how the forces of nature will not be defeated by forces of evil.

Just as in Oklahoma where the survivor's tree stands guard
over the site where violence and death occurred
and shouts to the power and presence of life,
so a tree stands guard over each of these stations
and over each of the stations that lead from the manger
to the mission that lies before us.
For this child, born in a manger,
the tree of the cross will guide and guard his every turn.
This tree, salvation's tree,
will make sure that what we celebrate at each of these stations
will come full circle
and create circles of hope, love and peace that will never end.

May we go then
in the peace and love and hope of our God!